MARK STALLARD

Published by Addax Publishing Group, Inc.

Edited by An Beard
Cover Designed by Laura Bolter
Text Designed by Mark Stallard
and Randy Breeden

For Information address:
Addax Publishing Group, Inc.
8643 Hauser Drive, Suite 235, Lenexa, KS 66215

ISBN: 1-886110-88-3

Library of Congress Cataloging-in-Publication Data

Stallard, Mark 1958-
AFL to Arrowhead : four decades of Chiefs history and trivia / by Mark Stallard.
p. cm.
ISBN 1-886110-88-3 (pbk.)
1. Kansas City Chiefs (Football team)--History. 2. Kansas City Chiefs (Football team)--Statistics. 3. Kansas City Chiefs (Football team)--Miscellanea. I. Title.

GV956.K35 S82 1999
796.332'64'0977844--dc21

99-047771

Printed in the USA

1 3 5 7 9 10 8 6 4 2

To Mom & Dad, who were always there;
and the 1969 Chiefs,
who showed what a team can do
with a second chance.

Let these fellows go their own way. If they succeed it will be good for football. If they fail it won't hurt the NFL.

George Halas
on the founders of the AFL

Winning is the yardstick...Everybody wants to go to the Super Bowl in July, everybody wants to go in December. But you have to want to go every day in between, too.

Len Dawson

Everything was wonderful to me in Kansas City...

Ernest Hemingway

Contents

CHIEFS NUMBERS

MORE TRIVIA

Acknowledgements

Working on a book like this always requires the help of a lot people, and I feel fortunate to have had many different research and football experts, photo suppliers and Chiefs fans in general contribute to and greatly enhance my efforts.

Thanks to Bob Snodgrass at Addax Publishing for believing in this book. Jim Donovan provided valuable help and guidance. I owe a big thank you to Alan Barzee who supplied many of the excellent photos in this book, as well as a lot of encouragement. An Beard's editorial expertise is greatly appreciated. Also, thank you to Nelson Elliott and the entire staff at Addax Publishing. Kristin Eshelman and the staff of the Kansas Collection at the University of Kansas set me free among a treasure of negatives. Her cheerful help was invaluable. Bern Ketchum and Jonell Muckenthaler at *The Topeka Capital-Journal* deserve many accolades for helping me. Special thanks to Tommy Brooker, ol' number 81, for his extra effort in supplying much needed material.

Others who helped with photos include: Curt Floerchinger of *The Kansas City Star*, Kevin Rettig at Corbis-Bettmann, Charles E. Brown of the St. Louis Mercantile Library, Mark Rucker of Transcendental Graphics, and Chris Watts of Tek Graphics. Many thanks to Janet Feltham and Sara Beckley of the Kansas City Chiefs for their efforts and help. Pete Fierle, Saleem Choudhry, and Bernadine Jenkins at the Pro Football Hall of Fame helped me find many different pieces of valuable research information. Lloyd Johnson, Bob Carroll, Keith Zimmerman and Bobby Plapinger also supplied some important items.

On a more personal note, thanks to Dan Consolver for his years of support, and Mike O'Connell, for his convincing stories about his high school football team. Larry Smith, Dick Woodward and Tom Shine taught me more things than I remember—thanks guys.

The biggest thanks go to my wife Merrie Jo. Her love and support are a big part of this book. I couldn't have done this without her.

Finally, I want to thank the Kansas City Chiefs for being such a classy organization and providing the fans of Kansas City with an exciting football team.

Introduction

I was just ten when I saw my first Chiefs game in the late summer of 1968, a pre-season matchup against the Oakland Raiders. Pro football was still new to me, so I wasn't prepared for the festive, rowdy atmosphere that engulfed Municipal Stadium before, during and after the game.

The defending AFL champs, Oakland had beaten the Chiefs twice the year before, which inspired vengeful contempt and loathing from the loud crowd. It was nonstop, nonsensical shouts; once the fans raised their voices, it seemed they never let up. And this was a *pre-season* game.

I don't remember who kicked off, but early in the first quarter Len Dawson threw a long touchdown pass to Otis Taylor for the game's first score. Minutes later Dawson tossed another touchdown pass to Frank Pitts, and a deafening delirium swept the stands. When Wendell Hayes scored on a one-yard run in the fourth quarter to put the Chiefs up 31-14, I thought the stadium would crumble beneath my feet. The hated Raiders were beaten. By game's end I hated them, too. Never mind it was only a preseason game. It didn't matter to the fans, and I don't think it mattered to the Kansas City players. Beating Oakland was always good. That night I learned Chiefs football was already a religion for Kansas City fans, and hating the Raiders was just another part of the ritual. Plus, it was fun. It's good to know that some things never change.

I left the stadium that night with a Chiefs bobber head doll and pennant, still the two greatest souvenirs I've ever gotten. The long journey of the 1968 season lay ahead of me, and with each passing week, I became more obsessed with—and addicted to—the team.

I was ecstatic when they won (although I'll admit I always *expected* the Chiefs to win), overly depressed when they lost (as much as a ten-year-old can be depressed), never believing for a moment they wouldn't win it all. Kansas City lost to the Jets by one point at Municipal, 20-19 (I didn't like Namath for a long time because of that one game), but ran the befuddled Raiders into the ground in the famous "T-formation" game at Municipal, winning 24-10.

Later in the season at Oakland, the Raiders ended the Chiefs' six-game winning streak, 38-21, a game that was much more lopsided than the score. Kansas City finished the season on a strong note though, pounding the Chargers and Broncos to run their record to 12-2, still the best in team history. But Oakland only lost two games, too, and a Divisional Playoff was setup. I was hopeful… .

The Raiders humiliated Kansas City, 41-6, to earn a spot in the AFL Championship Game against the Jets.

I'm not sure what lessons the 1968 season taught me, if any, except maybe patience and forgiveness. But it's those reasons, and maybe because they were the first team I really cared about, that made the '68 Chiefs my all-time favorite football team. To this day I wish they could have played the Colts in Super Bowl III instead of the Jets.

Combing through the lost pieces of the Chiefs history to put this book together revived many of my best memories of football. 1968 wasn't the Chiefs' year, but they got another chance. Kansas City beat their two nemeses, New York and Oakland, in the playoffs the following year, and while they didn't get a shot at Baltimore, it didn't matter. The Chiefs Super Bowl IV triumph over Minnesota remains for me, like all Kansas City fans who experienced it in 1970, the foremost and best of memories.

* * *

The task of chronicling the Chiefs' history, finding quality photos and pulling together more than 500 trivia questions proved monumental. Highlighting the Chiefs' best players and seasons was important, but I also wanted some of the forgotten players and moments from the franchise's past to find a place in the book as well. I think I've done that.

I hope you enjoy *AFL to Arrowhead*.

M.S.

Chiefs History

Goin' to Kansas City
A Brief History of the Chiefs

I was impressed with Mayor Bartle. He spoke highly of Kansas City... We were looking for a home where we would be welcome, and he just made me feel that we could do well in Kansas City.

Lamar Hunt
on moving the Dallas Texans to KC

There was never supposed to be a Kansas City franchise in the AFL, not one owned by the league's founder anyway. The Texans were the prize Lamar Hunt wanted and pursued—a pro football team in Dallas. But after three seasons of head-to-head competition with the NFL's Cowboys, it was apparent the Texans were failing to capture the majority of the fans in the Dallas—which also meant they were failing financially. So despite winning the AFL Championship in 1962, the following spring Hunt announced the team would move to Kansas City and be renamed the Chiefs.

Super Bowl Champs! Lamar Hunt, Otis Taylor, Hank Stram, Len Dawson and Bill Grigsby show off the Super Bowl IV trophy at a rally following the Chiefs' victory over the Vikings.

This inauspicious beginning in Kansas City as a castoff, throw-away team from another city was hard for the Chiefs to overcome their first couple of seasons. But the franchise ultimately thrived, and its history is rich with extraordinary successes. Knowing the club has also endured more than its share of tragedy and loss, the triumphs and victories stand bigger still. This was a franchise that refused to fail.

That the team exists at all is a lasting tribute to Lamar Hunt and his dream to own a pro football team. The improbable gamble of starting a new league not only succeeded, but forever changed the game of pro football, on and off the field. And Kansas City has been the greatest beneficiary of Hunt's vision.

The NFL Says No

Lamar Hunt began his pursuit of bringing professional football to Dallas in 1958. An NFL franchise had failed in the Texas city as recently as 1952, but the then 26-year-old SMU graduate was convinced that given the right opportunity, not only would a professional team succeed in Dallas, it would flourish.

He began his odyssey to obtain a football franchise in Chicago, hoping to purchase the Chicago Cardinals (who eventually moved to St. Louis in 1960, and from St. Louis to Arizona in 1988). But the team wasn't for sale. He then talked to various league officials, "Papa Bear" George Halas and Commissioner Bert Bell to name a couple, concerning the possibility of obtaining an expansion franchise for Dallas. Hunt was unceremoniously turned down. He was told that there would not be now, or maybe ever, expansion in the NFL. Period.

The Foolish Club

The concept of a new professional football league, Hunt has said, just came to him after he heard several other men were interested in either buying the Cardinals or getting an NFL expansion franchise themselves. And if so many were interested in owning an NFL team, he reasoned, they might be interested in forming a new league.

The Dallas Texans Team Logo

Hunt assembled a group of prospective owners, dubbed the "Foolish Club" by Wayne Valley, part of Oakland's owner group, and the

American Football League was born. The original six owners were Bud Adams in Houston; Cal Kunz in Denver; Lamar Hunt in Dallas; Harry Wismer in New York; Chet Soda led the group in Oakland; and Barron Hilton in Los Angeles. Billy Sullivan in Boston and Ralph Wilson in Buffalo were later added to the league.

Lamar Hunt

Once the owners and cities of the league were in place, Hunt began the process of building his franchise. He named the club the Texans (which was also the name of the failed NFL team in 1952) and chose an unknown assistant coach from the University of Miami, Hank Stram, as the team's

Some Memorable Moments in Chiefs History

- Abner Haynes scoring 19 touchdowns in the 1962 season
- Winning the 1962 AFL title as the Texans
- Playing the Packers in Super Bowl I
- Hank Stram's use of the "T" formation against the Raiders in 1968
- Winning the last AFL Championship game against the Raiders
- Mike Garrett's touchdown run in Super Bowl IV
- Len Dawson connecting with Otis Taylor for a touchdown in Super Bowl IV
- Jan Stenerud booting a 55-yard field goal
- Ed Podolak's outstanding one-man rampage in the 1971 Divisional Playoff game against Miami
- Lamar Hunt being inducted into the Pro Football Hall of Fame in 1972
- Returning to the playoffs in 1986
- Nick Lowery's two club record 58-yard field goals
- Christian Okoye breaking the club's all-time rushing record
- Marty Schottenheimer coming to Kansas City
- Derrick Thomas' seven quarterback sacks in one game
- Joe Montana's game-tying touchdown pass in the 1993 First Round Playoff game against the Steelers
- Marcus Allen setting the NFL record for rushing touchdowns in 1997
- Pete Stoyanovich's 54-yard game-winning field goal vs. Denver in 1997

head coach. It was an excellent choice. The stocky, robust Stram would lead the franchise for 15 seasons and be the major architect of its finest moments.

Sherrill Headrick

To create strong local interest and foster team identity with the fans, Hunt made sure the Texans were stocked with lots of college talent from Texas. Abner Haynes, from North Texas State, quickly became the team's — and league's — marquee player. Other top Texas players added to the roster the first couple of seasons included Jack Spikes, E.J. Holub, Sherrill Headrick, and Jerry Mays.

When the NFL announced it was expanding into Dallas and Minnesota, it was a move Hunt hadn't considered or accounted for, and one that ultimately led to problems.

"This is an effort to sabotage us that will be apparent to 170 million people," Hunt said of the NFL's tactics. Maybe he knew even then that Dallas simply wasn't big enough to be a two-team town.

Pro Football in Texas

The Dallas Texans began their first season with a loss to the Chargers, 21-20. Appropriately, the team's first-ever win came against the Raiders at Oakland, 34-16. But the team never really got going, and despite the star quality and outstanding play of Abner Haynes, the Texans finished their inaugural campaign with an 8-6 record. They slipped to 6-8 in 1961, but good things were about to happen. A little used and somewhat floundering quarterback in the NFL arrived for the 1962 season. He would became the shining light of the team for the next 14 seasons. His name was Len Dawson.

Hank Stram

With Dawson running the offense,

the Texans won their first Western Division title in 1962 finishing with an 11-3 record. They met the Oilers in Houston for the AFL Championship, a game that was to become a classic and one of the AFL's early defining moments. Dallas "won" the first half of the game, scoring 17 unanswered points. Houston claimed the second half, scoring 17 points of their own. The two teams battled into a second overtime period before Dallas claimed the championship on a 25-yard field goal by Tommy Brooker. The Texans were ready to claim Dallas for their own.

But the reality of the Texans' situation couldn't be ignored. So despite winning the championship and the apparent maturation by the AFL as a whole toward stability and respectability, the financial facts surrounding the Texans were obvious. Hunt couldn't compete with the NFL's Cowboys and was going to have to move the Texans. After making a preliminary statement in February, 1963, he made it official in May — the Texans were going to Kansas City.

"We had been so wrapped up in trying to win football games," said Hank Stram, "that most of us had never given any thought to the possibility of the team being moved."

The Kansas City Texans?

Once the announcement that Dallas was moving to Kansas City was made, Hunt made it known that he very much wanted to keep the name Texans for the team. Hunt felt there wasn't a decision to make—he was determined to keep the name. Imagine, the Kansas City Texans of the American Football League. Hunt came to the realization, or maybe his senses, that a team called the Texans must reside in the Lone Star State, and he eventually listened to General Manager Jack Steadman, who talked him out of keeping the name.

The Kansas City Star ran a name contest for the city's new franchise, and from suggestions that included Mules, Stars, Royals and Steers, the name Chiefs was chosen in part, Hunt explained, to honor the Indian tribes in the Kansas City region, and also as a tribute to Kansas City's mayor, H. Roe Bartle, who was known as "Chief."

Kansas City Chiefs Original Team Logo

Turmoil and Tragedy

Most of the Texans players resented and resisted the move from Dallas. As the defending AFL champs, they couldn't understand why the Texans were leaving instead of the then lowly NFL Cowboys. It was this prevailing attitude that made for a difficult transition.

Fred Arbanas

But whether they were the Texans or Chiefs, the franchise was still a championship team, and much was expected of them. Then tragedy stepped in.

In the final exhibition game before the 1963 season started, Chiefs rookie flanker and former Olympian Stone Johnson broke his neck and died less than two weeks later. It was a tremendous blow to the team. Johnson had already won over his teammates and promised to be a star. His death was the first of several unfortunate and tragic moments that came to visit the Chiefs during their first three seasons in Kansas City.

Guard Ed Budde suffered a fractured skull and Fred Arbanas lost

Len Dawson sets up to pass against the Green Bay Packers in the first Super Bowl.

vision in his left eye. Both players careers were in doubt; luckily, both were able to return and continue their strong contributions to the team.

The worst of the tragedies was the death of star fullback Mack Lee Hill, who died during routine knee surgery at the end of the 1965 season. Hill had already established himself as a great, crunching runner, and his best years appeared to be ahead of him. Once again the Chiefs were devastated; still they finished with a 7-5-2 record, the best since the team moved from Dallas. When they were able to put Hill's death behind them, the Chiefs looked for good things to happen.

The First Super Bowl

The significance of 1966 was twofold. First, the team finally achieved the kind of success that had been expected of them when they first came to Kansas City and became what they always thought they were; the best team in the league. More importantly, the Chiefs were finally and forever taken to the hearts of Kansas City's fans. And when the Chiefs thumped Buffalo, 31-7, in the 1966 AFL Championship Game, they earned the right to play the NFL champion Green Bay Packers in the first-ever AFL-NFL World Championship Game (not yet officially called the Super Bowl) in Los Angeles, the initial step of the two leagues ultimate merger, which would occur in 1970.

The first Super Bowl matchup was a curiosity to the American public, but not much more. Green Bay was heavily favored, and 30,000 seats went unsold at the Los Angeles Colosseum. The Chiefs stayed with the Packers in the first half, but a costly interception early in the third period turned the tide for the Packers, and they waltzed to a 35-10 win.

"I sincerely felt we could win," Stram said after the game. "And I think our people felt that way."

The Super Team

It took the Chiefs two years to rebuild and make a another run at the Super Bowl, and the team experienced a few hard knocks getting there.

A devastating playoff loss to the Raiders ended the 1968 season, but the Chiefs players—and Stram in particular—felt they had the kind of team needed to return to make a run at the Super Bowl. Jim Marsalis, the club's top draft pick in 1969, took over the left cornerback spot and immediately improved the secondary on an already strong defense.

Chiefs' Super Bowl IV Shoulder Patch

Johnny Robinson flips after recovering a fumble in Super Bowl IV. Jim Marsalis (number 40 on ground), Bobby Bell and Willie Lanier look on.

The Chiefs overcame several injuries throughout the 1969 season, specifically the one to Len Dawson's knee, and again challenged the Raiders for the Western Division title. A 10-6 loss at Oakland in the season's final game, their second loss to the Raiders that season, left the Chiefs with an 11-3 record and another second place finish in the division. But because of a one-time-only playoff format implemented by the AFL for its final season, the Chiefs were still in the hunt for the Super Bowl. To make it to New Orleans for the big game, the Chiefs had to beat the defending world champion Jets in New York, and if they accomplished that, upset the Raiders in Oakland. Willie Lanier and the defense led the way in New York as the Chiefs fought through the bitter cold and beat the Jets, 13-6. Two weeks later the team defied the odds and surprised the football world, as well as the Raiders, to win the final AFL championship in Oakland, 17-7, to return to the Super Bowl.

Super Bowl IV

Once again the Chiefs were heavy underdogs when they took the field at Tulane Stadium in New Orleans for Super Bowl IV. But unlike the game against the Packers, the Chiefs felt they would win. Len Dawson shook off false gambling accusations and played a superb game to capture MVP honors. Jan Stenerud booted three field goals for Kansas City, Mike Garrett scored a touchdown, and Otis Taylor put the game away with a spectacular 46-yard scoring reception. The Chiefs dominated the

Mike Garrett, Gloster Richardson and Otis Taylor celebrate Garrett's touchdown run in Super Bowl IV.

Vikings from start to finish, 23-7, and won Super Bowl IV.

The Longest Game

The Chiefs emerged from the 1960s as the most successful team in AFL history and seemed primed to do the same in the NFL. But after proclaiming his offense as the "Offense of the Seventies" following the Super Bowl win, Stram wasn't able to maintain the high level of play from the Chiefs. After slipping slightly in 1970, the team rebounded in 1971 to again win the AFC West. Kansas City hosted Miami in a Divisional Playoff game on Christmas Day, and for the second time in the franchise's history, battled in a double-overtime marathon. After more than 82 minutes of playing time, Miami finally won the longest game in NFL history, 27-24. The game marked the end of Municipal Stadium, and also the end of the Chiefs as a league power.

Chiefs cornerback, Jim Marsalis, plays it tight against the Raiders' Fred Biletnikoff.

The Losing Years

The Chiefs slipped a lot and fell to 5-9 in 1974. Hunt and Steadman decided it was time to make a change. After 15 years as the Chiefs head coach, Hank Stram was fired, a move which ignited a chain reaction that had been building for two seasons. The Chiefs spiraled into a dismal free-fall to the bottom of the NFL. After winning their division in 1971 and posting winning records in 1972-73, Kansas City won just 23 games from 1975 through 1979. Stram's successor, Paul Wiggin, was fired in the middle of the 1977 season, as the Chiefs finished with the

Tony Reed

FIGHTING WORDS

I don't like the Chiefs, and I hope they hear what I'm saying. I have an intense hatred for them.

Marv Hubbard
Raiders fullback, 1969-75

Each game has always been a monumental one. If they (Raiders) beat us twice, they'd damn near gotten the league wrapped up. And if we beat them twice, we'd done the same thing.

Willie Lanier
Chiefs linebacker, 1967-77

We're like tough old partners of an unhappy marriage, each knowing just where to kick, scratch and scream to cause each other the most anguish.

Jim Otto
Raiders center, 1960-74

Great teams produce great rivalries, and the annual Chiefs-Raiders matchups are the best in the NFL. Since the beginning of the AFL these two teams have, for lack of better words, hated one another; really despised the other team. When the Chiefs won the 1966 AFL Championship, they pounded the Raiders in Oakland, but got embarrassed at home. And when the Raiders went 13-1 in 1967, including two big wins against Kansas City, the rivalry reached a boiling point and has never stopped simmering. The Raiders won most of the games in the series throughout the 1970s and 1980s, but the Chiefs have owned the Raiders throughout the 1990s. Kansas City's dominance hasn't diminished the rivalry—there is still nothing as satisfying to Chiefs fans as a win over Oakland.

Derrick Thomas pressures the Raiders' Jeff Hostetler.

franchise's worst-ever record at 2-12. Marv Levy took the head coaching position next, and while he was able to bring a mediocre respectability to the Chiefs, he was fired after five up and down seasons.

Tragedy again struck the Chiefs when their star running back Joe Delaney drowned while trying to rescue three young boys from a pond near his home in Monroe, Louisiana. Delaney had been the best player to join the Chiefs in more than a decade. His death took a huge emotional toll on the team.

John Mackovic took over from Levy and despite the loss of Delaney, slowly rebuilt the team into a contender. His fourth year as head coach reaped a playoff berth as the Chiefs finished 10-6, winning many games on the spectacular play of their special teams (11 blocked kicks and 6 touchdown returns). It was the club's first post-season spot in 15 years. The Chiefs lost in the first round to the Jets, but the promise of more playoffs seemed bright. But the new-found success was short-lived. After a series of political maneuvers between players, management and assistant coaches, Hunt and Steadman fired Mackovic. His replacement was his special teams coach, Frank Gansz. This move proved to be especially disastrous, and the team again plummeted to the bottom the NFL.

Christian Okoye runs against the Packers in a 1987 game.

Steve DeBerg shows frustration coming off the field in the 1990 Playoff Game against Miami.

Marty Ball

When Gansz produced only eight wins in two seasons, Hunt again made major changes. He replaced Steadman with Carl Peterson, who became the new President/General Manager/CEO of the team. Peterson's first order of business was giving Gansz the boot and hiring Marty Schottenheimer as the team's new head coach.

Nick Lowery watches after booting the game-winning field goal in the '93 Playoff against the Steelers.

"I believe the opportunity is there with this football team to once again approach that great tradition of the Kansas City Chiefs," said Schottenheimer when named head coach. "My principal reason for selecting this opportunity is that I believe we can win—and win very, very quickly." He was right—the results of Schottenheimer's coaching techniques were immediate and amazing.

After years of regularly fielding non-competitive teams, the Chiefs began to win consistently. Led by Christian Okoye, the NFL's top rusher, the Chiefs just missed a playoff spot in 1989. They posted an 11-5 mark in 1990 and made the playoffs,

Joe Montana and Marty Schottenheimer discuss strategy during the 1993 playoff game with the Steelers.

the first of six consecutive trips to post-season play for Kansas City. The downside of this new success was the team's playoff performance, winning just one of four playoff games from 1990 through 1992.

Joe Montana and Marcus Allen

Searching for the final pieces to the Super Bowl puzzle, the Chiefs traded for legendary quarterback Joe Montana and signed free agent running back Marcus Allen prior to the 1993 season. The two superstars were near the end of their careers, but coming to the Chiefs revitalized both. Behind the two stars, Kansas City captured the 1993 AFC Western Division title with an 11-5 record and won two playoff games. The Chiefs appeared in their first-ever AFC Championship game at Buffalo, but when Montana had to leave the game with a concussion early in the third quarter, the Chiefs were unable to rally and lost, 30-13.

Marcus Allen runs against his former team, the Raiders.

Montana retired following the 1994 season, and Steve Bono took over the quarterbacking duties. The 1995 Chiefs rode their defense to an NFL-best record 13-3, but suffered an embarrassing upset loss at home to the Colts in the playoffs. In 1996 the Chiefs failed to make the playoffs for the first time in seven years.

Elvis in the House

By signing Elvis Grbac, the Chiefs were hoping to finally have a long-term quarterback, a guy that would be around for more than a couple of seasons. Interestingly, Grbac was the third straight quarterback to come to the Chiefs from the 49ers.

The 1997 Chiefs matched the 1995 team's 13-3 record, went undefeated at Arrowhead and again captured home-field advantage throughout the playoffs.The defense was dominating, and spurred by a close 24-22 win over the Broncos at Arrowhead, the Chiefs again won the AFC West. But like the '95 club, the '97 Chiefs couldn't take advantage of their NFL-best record. They dropped a close contest in the Divisional Playoff to the

Chiefs in the NFL Hall of Fame. From the left, Bobby Bell, Lamar Hunt, Willie Lanier (behind Hunt), Len Dawson, Buck Buchanan and Jan Stenerud.

Broncos, 14-10, ending an otherwise brilliant season.

The Chiefs exploded against the Raiders in the first game of the 1998 season, and after fighting the rain and wind in many of their games, fashioned a 4-1 record to start the season and looked to again be in a position to challenge for the division title. A 40-10 thrashing at the hands of the Patriots set the team in the opposite direction. Kansas City dropped six games in a row and finished the season 7-9, Schottenheimer's first losing season ever as a head coach in the NFL. The real shocker came on January 11, 1999, when Schottenheimer suddenly announced he was retiring.

Less than two weeks later Peterson hired Chiefs defensive coordinator Gunther Cunningham as the team's eighth head coach, and a new era of Chiefs football started. Determined to get to the Super Bowl, Peterson revamped the secondary, beefed up the linebackers, and signed veteran quarterback Warren Moon to back up Grbac. Armed with new players, a strong work ethic and great leadership, Cunningham would try to re-establish the Chiefs as one of the NFL's elite teams.

Elvis Grbac in the '97 Playoff Game against Denver.

Chiefs Chronology

The early history of the Chiefs is also the history of the American Football League. The original eight franchises in the league were bound together by more than games and rivalries—each team's success directly depended on the success of the other teams in the league; what affected one team affected all. For this reason, some pertinent dates in the development, growth and eventual merger of the AFL and NFL are included with the important dates in the Chiefs history.

1958

Fall - Lamar Hunt starts his pursuit of a professional football team. He checks out the possibility of buying the Chicago Cardinals, and also speaks with NFL commissioner Bert Bell about expansion. But the Cardinals aren't for sale, and the NFL says expansion will not happen any time soon, if ever. When Hunt hears of other parties interested in buying or expanding into the NFL, he conceives the idea of starting a new league.

1959

Spring - Hunt assembles a group of owners for the new league.

August 14 - The first organizational meeting for the new professional football league is held. League founder Lamar Hunt heads the gathering. Teams will be in New York, Dallas, Los Angeles, Minneapolis, Denver and Houston. Buffalo and Boston join later in the fall and Oakland eventually replaces Minneapolis. League play will start in 1960.

August 22 - Second league meeting. American Football League (AFL) is chosen as the name for the new league.

November 22 - The first AFL player draft is held. The Texans choose Don Meredith, quarterback from SMU, as their first round pick. Meredith later signed with the Cowboys.

November 30 - Joe Foss is named commissioner of the AFL.

Lamar Hunt

1960

January 26 - Lamar Hunt is named the first league president.

June 9 - The AFL signs a five-year TV package with ABC.

June 17 - The AFL files a $10 million antitrust suit against the NFL.

> *It was sort of like a light bulb coming on. I got to thinking... maybe there was enough interest nationwide to form a new league.*
> **Lamar Hunt**

July 8 - The Dallas Texans open their first training camp.

July 31 - The Texans play their first game ever, an exhibition win over the Raiders, 20-13.

August 25 - The AFL adopts a league resolution to have player names on the back of their jerseys.

September 9 - First game of the AFL. Denver defeats Boston, 13-10.

September 10 - The Texans lose their first game to the Chargers in Los Angeles, 21-20.

November 24 - Abner Haynes racks up 157 yards rushing against the Titans in New York, but the Texans still lose, 41-35.

December 18 - The Texans defeat Buffalo, 24-7, ending their first season with an 8-6 record and second place finish in the Western Division. Abner Haynes wins the rushing title and is named Rookie-of-the-Year, as well as Outstanding Player in the AFL.

1961

February 10 - The Chargers are given permission to move from Los Angeles to San Diego.

September 10 - The Texans open the season with a 26-10 loss at home to the Chargers.

October 8 - The Texans defeat the Broncos in Denver, 19-12, the team's third win in a row.

Abner Haynes flies into the end zone for the Dallas Texans as quarterback Cotton Davidson (19) and a lot of empty seats look on.

November 3 - The Texans comeback is thwarted by a fan on the field. Cotton Davidson's last-second pass is knocked down by a spectator in the end zone. Surprisingly, the officials let the play stand and the Texans lose at Boston, 28-21.

November 26 - Abner Haynes sets a team record by scoring five touchdowns, four of them rushing, in the Texans 43-11 pounding of the Raiders at the Cotton Bowl. The win snaps a six-game losing streak.

December 17 - The end of a disappointing season. The Texans triumph over the New York Titans, 35-24, but still end the season with a losing record, 6-8, and a second place finish in the Western Division.

Tommy Brooker is carried off the field by teammates Fred Arbanas and Bobby Hunt after kicking the game-winning field goal in the 1962 AFL Championship game.

1962

January 7 - First AFL All-Star game. The West defeats the East, 47-27. Dallas quarterback Cotton Davidson is named Most Outstanding Player of the game.

Summer - Len Dawson signs with the Texans.

June 27 - AFL owners vote to defer league expansion until a later date. Cities under consideration included Kansas City, New Orleans and Atlanta.

September 8 - The Texans open the season with a 42-28 win over Boston at the Cotton Bowl.

September 30 - Abner Haynes rushes for 164 yards on 16 carries as the Texans romp over the Bills, 41-21.

October 12 - Len Dawson passes for 302 yards and two touchdowns as the Texans beat the Patriots, 27-7, in Boston. Chris Burford catches 10 passes for 171 receiving yards.

November 18 - Len Dawson and Tommy Brooker hook up on a 92-yard touchdown pass as the Texans beat the Broncos, 24-3.

December 1 - Using the draft choice they received from Oakland in the Cotton Davidson trade, the Texans choose Buck Buchanan of Grambling College as the number one pick in the AFL draft and sign him immediately.

December 16 - Dallas wins the season finale, beating the Chargers, 26-17, at the Cotton Bowl. The Texans finish with an 11-3 record and first place in the AFL West.

> *Don't worry about it. It's all over now.*
>
> **Tommy Brooker, 1962**
> to his teammates before his game-winning kick in the AFL Championship game

December 23 - AFL Champs! The Texans win a thrilling double-overtime game against the Houston Oilers and claim their first league championship, 20-17. Tommy Brooker's 25-yard field goal ended what was at that time pro football's longest game at 77 minutes and 54 seconds. Texans back Jack Spikes rushed for 77 yards to earn game MVP honors. Abner Haynes scored two touchdowns.

The 1962 Dallas Texans
American Football League Champions

1963

January 13 - West defeats East 21-14 in the second AFL All-Star game at San Diego. Texans running back Curtis McClinton is named Outstanding Offensive Player of the game.

February 8 - Lamar Hunt announces he will move the Texans from Dallas to Kansas City if the city can meet guaranteed season ticket sales, expand Municipal Stadium and build new team offices and practice facilities.

May 14 - It's official. Hunt announces he is moving the Texans to Kansas City. The team is renamed the Kansas City Chiefs.

August 9 - First game in Kansas City. Before an extremely small crowd of 5,721 "Show-Me-State" spectators, the Chiefs debut at Municipal Stadium, beating Buffalo, 17-13, in an exhibition game.

August 31 - In their final pre-season game in Wichita, Kansas, the Chiefs lose to Houston, 23-17. In the game, Stone Johnson, a rookie flanker from Grambling, injures his neck and is paralyzed. He dies on September 8, a tragedy that affects the team for the rest of the season.

> *It is the most tragic thing that has happened to us since we started the organization. Johnson was a great athlete and a fine gentleman.*
>
> **Jack Steadman**
> on Stone Johnson's death

September 7 - The Chiefs debut in the regular season as a Kansas City team with a 59-7 rout of the Broncos in Denver. The 59 points scored is the most ever by a Chiefs team in a regular season game.

October 6 - A crowd of 27,801 cheers on the Chiefs in their home opener. They go home happy as the Chiefs defeat the Oilers, 28-7.

November 24 - All AFL games are postponed following the assassination of President Kennedy. The NFL plays their games and is highly criticized.

Stone Johnson

December 22 - The Chiefs beat the Jets, 48-0, and end their first season in Kansas City with a disappointing record of 5-7-2.

1964

January 29 - The AFL and NBC sign a five-year TV contract worth $36 million. NBC begins broadcasting games in 1965.

March 6 - Chiefs offensive guard Ed Budde is injured in a fight and suffers a fractured skull. He isn't given clearance to play until training camp opens.

Ed Budde

September 13 - Kansas City opens the season at Buffalo and loses, 34-17.

October 4 - First home game of the year. The Chiefs beat the Oilers, 28-7, before only 22,727 fans.

November 1 - Len Dawson passes for a club record 435 yards and six touchdowns as the Chiefs down the Broncos, 49-39, at Municipal Stadium. "Lenny the Cool" hit on 23 of 38 attempts.

December 13 - The Chiefs rout the Chargers in San Diego, 49-6.

December 20 - The Jets beat the Chiefs at Municipal, 24-7. Kansas City finishes the season with a 7-7 record, second in the AFL West.

December - Chiefs tight end Fred Arbanas is attacked by an unknown mugger and suffers major damage to his left eye. Despite losing almost all vision in the eye, Arbanas returns the following year and continues his career.

1965

January 2 - Alabama quarterback Joe Namath signs a $400,000 contract with the New York Jets, the largest amount ever paid to a graduating collegian.

June 7 - The AFL votes to expand by two teams. Miami is later awarded the league's first expansion franchise, and Cincinnati will eventually receive the second.

Mack Lee Hill

September 12 - The Raiders pound the Chiefs in the season opener at Oakland, 37-10.

October 3 - Kansas City beats the Patriots at Municipal, 27-17.

October 31 - Revenge on the Raiders. The Chiefs beat Oakland at home, 14-7.

November 28 - Houston is routed by the Chiefs, 52-21. Mack Lee Hill rumbles for 119 yards.

December 14 - Mack Lee Hill, the Chiefs' star second-year fullback, dies during knee surgery. He injured the knee against Buffalo two days earlier and died when his body temperature soared to 108 degrees during the surgery. His death devastates the team.

> *He fulfilled every expectation this year and earned the respect and admiration of his coaches, teammates and every team in the AFL. He was probably one of the most unselfish players I have ever coached.*
>
> **Hank Stram**
> on Mack Lee Hill

December 19 - The Chiefs end the season with a 45-35 win over the Broncos at Municipal Stadium to finish with a 7-5-2 record. Curtis McClinton catches five passes for 213 yards in the win.

1966

April 8 - Al Davis, Raiders general manager, is voted in as the new commissioner of the AFL.

June 8 - The AFL and NFL announce the two leagues have agreed to a merger. A championship game between the two leagues will take place and the two leagues would share a common player draft. Starting in 1970, the two leagues will become one, a larger NFL.

July 25 - The merger complete, Al Davis resigns as the AFL's commissioner.

September 11 - The Chiefs open the season with a romp of the Bills, 42-20, in Buffalo.

October 23 - The Chiefs annihilate the Broncos at Denver, 56-10. The convincing win sets up the rest of the season and improves the team's mark to 5-2.

October 30 - Otis Taylor catches five passes for 187 yards as the Chiefs roll to a 48-23 win over the Oilers at Municipal.

November 27 - The Chiefs clinch the AFL West title. Kansas City defeats the Jets, 32-24, in New York to capture the franchise's second division title.

December 18 - The Chiefs wrap up the regular season with a 27-17 win at San Diego. Kansas City finishes with an 11-2-1 record. Eleven Chiefs are selected for the West Division All-Stars.

1967

January 1 - AFL Champs again. Playing in frigid conditions, the Chiefs roll past the Bills in Buffalo, 31-7, and capture the AFL championship. Mike Garrett scores two touchdowns and Len Dawson throws a couple of touchdown passes to lead the offense.

> *I smashed him on the head and they missed a first down by inches...The hammer, we got the hammer!*
>
> **Fred Williamson**
> after 1966 AFL Title game

January 15 - Super Sunday Number One. The Chiefs take their place in history as the first AFL representative in what is now called Super Bowl I, but that's all they take as the Packers soundly defeat them, 35-10. Trailing just 14-10 at the half, Kansas City is unable to solve Green Bay's blitzing

Mike Mercer kicks a 32-yard field goal in the 1966 AFL Championship game.

Len Dawson prepares to hand off in 1966 AFL Title game.

Willie Mitchell of the Chiefs knocks the ball away from Green Bay's Carroll Dale as Fred Williamson looks on in Super Bowl I.

tactics and fails to move the ball with any consistency the rest of the game. Curtis McClinton scores the team's only touchdown.

March 14 - First AFL-NFL draft. The Chiefs selected Gene Trosch, defensive lineman from the University of Miami, as their number one pick. The team picked up Willie Lanier and Jim Lynch in the second round.

> *We are playing this game for every team, every player, every coach and every official in the AFL.*
>
> **Hank Stram**
> before Super Bowl I

August 23 - NFL ambushed. Hungry for revenge and redemption for their loss to Green Bay in the first Super Bowl, the Chiefs destroy the Chicago Bears at Municipal Stadium, 66-24, in a pre-season game. "This proves we're capable of winning any time we play anyone," Hank Stram said following the game.

> *All right. Kansas City doesn't compare with the top teams in the National Football League. That's what you wanted me to say—and now I've said it.*
>
> **Vince Lombardi**
> **Green Bay Head Coach**
> after Packers defeated Chiefs in Super Bowl I

October 8 - The Chiefs play their first home game of the season and pound the Dolphins, 41-0. The win moves their record to 3-1.

November 5 - The Chiefs crush the Jets at home, 42-18. Mike Garrett racks up 193 yards rushing in the win.

December 17 - Noland "Super Gnat" Smith returns a kickoff an NFL record 106 yards against the Broncos in Denver. The Chiefs win, 38-24, and end the season with a disappointing 9-5 record and second place finish in the AFL West.

1968

September 9 - The Chiefs open the season with a 26-21 win at Houston.

September 15 - The Chiefs lose, 20-19, to the Jets at home, a loss that will haunt them the rest of the season and ultimately keep them from winning the division. Jets quarterback Joe Namath controls the ball the final five and a half minutes of the game to seal the win for New York.

"Super Gnat"

October 20 - Injuries to the wide receiving corp force Coach Stram to alter his normal game plan—he installs the "T" formation and runs the Raiders to death. By the time Oakland makes the proper defensive adjustments, it's too late. The Chiefs win, 24-10, at Municipal, and set a record for the fewest passes thrown in an AFL game with just three. Garrett runs for 109 yards, Robert Holmes 95 yards and Wendell Hayes 89 yards.

November 3 - Oakland handles the Chiefs and wins, 38-21. Len Dawson hits Gloster Richardson for a 92-yard touchdown pass in the game.

December 14 - The Chiefs wrap up the regular season with a 30-7 win at Denver and finish with a 12-2 record. But the Raiders also finish at 12-2—a Divisional Playoff in Oakland awaits the Chiefs.

December 22 - The Raiders humiliate the Chiefs, 41-6, to win the Western Division and the right to play the Jets for the AFL Championship. The Raiders score touchdowns three of the first four times they have the ball. At the time it is the Chiefs worst defeat ever.

> *What do you think? The score was 41-6.*
>
> **Buck Buchanan**
> when asked if the Chiefs got the pass rush they wanted in the 1968 Western Division playoff

1969

January 12 - The AFL Champion New York Jets upset the Baltimore Colts in Super Bowl III, the AFL's first victory over the NFL in the championship game.

July - Stram bans all facial and long hair. Any player not complying faces a $500 fine.

September 14 - The Chiefs open the season at San Diego and dispose of the Chargers, 27-9.

September 21 - Kansas City defeats the Patriots in Boston, 31-0, but Dawson suffers an injury to his left knee. He misses several games.

September 28 - Dawson's backup Jacky Lee goes down, leaving the quarterbacking duties to Mike Livingston, a little-used third-string quarterback from SMU. The Chiefs fall to the Bengals in Cincinnati, 24-19.

Mike Livingston

October 19 - Mike Livingston, Otis Taylor and Robert Holmes combine for a 93-yard touchdown pass play. Taylor catches the pass and laterals to Holmes, who carries the ball into the end zone. The Chiefs beat the Dolphins, 17-10.

November 2 - Dawson returns to the lineup and the Chiefs win, stopping the Bills in Buffalo, 29-7.

November 16 - Kansas City destroys the defending World Champion New York Jets, 34-16, at Shea Stadium. The win is the seventh in a row for the team.

November 23 - The winning streak ends as the Chiefs fall to the Raiders at home, 27-24. The Chiefs outplay the Raiders statistically, but miscues and turnovers prove too much to overcome.

December 7 - Jan Stenerud hits five field goals as the Chiefs eke out a 22-19 win over the Bills in Kansas City.

December 13 - The Raiders defeat the Chiefs again, 10-6, at Oakland to clinch the AFL Western Division title. Kansas City attempts only six passes, and finishes the season with an 11-3 mark. But thanks to a special one-year-only setup, the Chiefs are in the playoffs for the Super Bowl.

December 20 - Using a ferocious goal-line stand in the fourth quarter, the Chiefs defeat the Jets, 13-6, to advance to the AFL Championship game. Dawson passes for 201 yards and a touchdown, and Jim Marsalis picks off two passes to lead the Chiefs.

The Chiefs were featured on the cover of *Sports Illustrated* after thrashing the Jets.

> *We have a lot to be proud of. Looking back over the years we've spent in the AFL, we've won three league championships. That's more than any other team.*
>
> **Lamar Hunt**

> *I don't think the Chiefs will be a good representative for the AFL (in the Super Bowl). I never did like Kansas City. I guess that's probably the reason I feel that way.*
>
> **Jim Otto, Raiders center**
> after 1969 AFL title game

1970

January 4 - Back to the Super Bowl. The Chiefs rode their defense to the title in the last AFL game ever, defeating the Raiders in Oakland, 17-7. Wendell Hayes and Robert Holmes each scored a touchdown, and Jan

Stenerud kicked a field goal late in the fourth quarter to seal the win. Emmitt Thomas picks off a couple of passes to lead a stingy defense.

January 11 - Super Chiefs! A poised, confident Chiefs team took the field at Tulane Stadium, and remembering the past lessons of a Super Bowl lost, took control of the game from the opening kickoff. The end result was a decisive Kansas City victory over the Minnesota Vikings, 23-7, in Super Bowl IV in New Orleans. The Chiefs are crowned World Champions of football. Representing the AFL in the league's last game ever, the Chiefs' win left the AFL-NFL tally at two games apiece. Despite being a two-touchdown underdog, KC never trailed in the game. Jan Stenerud booted three field goals, the longest from 48 yards, and Mike Garrett scampered into the end zone on a five-yard run to put KC up 16-0 at the half. Otis Taylor scored on a spectacular 46-yard pass play to close out the scoring and the defense man-handled Vikings quarterback Joe Kapp the rest of the game.

Hank Stram takes a victory ride after Super Bowl IV.

The 1969 Kansas City Chiefs World Champions.

Super Bowl IV MVP Len Dawson.

Len Dawson calls a play during Super Bowl IV.

Len Dawson, ignoring false gambling allegations that were made earlier in the week, played brilliantly and was named the game's MVP.

April 15 - Season ticket sales for Arrowhead Stadium begin, which eventually results in an NFL record 70,000 tickets.

July 31 - As the defending World Champions, the Chiefs take on the College All-Stars in Chicago and win easily, 24-3.

Bobby Bell wraps up a Colts runner in the Chiefs first *Monday Night Football* game.

September 20 - Vikings revenge. In a Super Bowl IV rematch, the Chiefs travel to Minnesota and are thumped, 27-10.

September 28 - In only the second telecast ever, the Chiefs make their first appearance on *Monday Night Football*, and whomp the Colts in Baltimore, 44-24.

October 4 - Jan Stenerud boots a 55-yard field goal in Denver, but the Chiefs lose, 26-13.

October 15 - Mike Garrett is traded to the Chargers for a second-round pick in the 1971 draft.

November 1 - With 1:08 left in the game, it appears the Chiefs have put the Raiders away and are going to win,17-14, and pull into a tie for first place in the AFC West. Dawson runs for what should be a game-winning first down, but an unnecessary roughness penalty by Raider Ben Davidson, followed by an ejection of Otis Taylor (he hit Davidson defending Dawson), and the Chiefs instead relinquish the ball, and ultimately, the lead. George Blanda kicks a 48-yard field goal with eight seconds left to tie the game at 17-17.

December 12 - With the division title again on the line, the Chiefs lose to the Raiders in Oakland, 20-6, and fail to make the playoffs.

December 20 - Kansas City loses the final game of the season at San Diego, 31-13, and finishes with a 7-5-2 record.

1971

September 19 - The Chiefs lose the season opener at San Diego, 21-14.

October 18 - On *Monday Night Football*, the Chiefs win easily against the Steelers at Municipal, 38-16.

October 24 - Kansas City vanquishes the Redskins, 27-20, the team's fifth win in a row.

October 31 - Those darn Raiders. The Raiders come from behind again, this time kicking a late field goal. The two rivals end the game in a tie, 20-20.

Ed Podolak takes a handoff from Len Dawson during 1971 action.

December 6 - The 49ers fall to the Chiefs on *Monday Night Football*, 26-17, setting the stage for a winner-take-all division championship game with Oakland.

December 12 - AFC Western Division Champs. Jan Stenerud kicks a late field goal set up by a Raider interference penalty to sneak by the Raiders, 16-14, and win the West. It is the Chiefs first division championship since 1966.

December 19 - Kansas City finishes the regular season with a 22-9 win over the Bills at Municipal, the first time in the club's history they finish a season undefeated at home. Their final record is 10-3-1.

> *I have the worst feeling anyone could have. I have no idea what I'm going to do now. I feel like hiding, I don't feel like playing football. It's a shame guys play like hell, like our team did, and lose because of a missed field goal. It's unbearable. It's totally unbearable.*
>
> **Jan Stenerud**
> after 1971 playoff loss

December 25 - Overtime history and heartbreak. The Chiefs come up short in the longest pro football game ever played and lose to the Dolphins, 27-24. Miami's Garo Yepremian boots a 37-yard field goal to end the double-overtime marathon after more than 82 minutes of playing time. Ed Podolak starred for the Chiefs, accumulating 350 all-purpose yards. The usually reliable Jan Stenerud added to the Chiefs' anguish, missing a field-goal attempt at the end of regulation that would have

Miami's Garo Yepremian (1)has just kicked his game-winning field goal in the 1971 Divisional Playoff. The Chiefs' Jim Kearney (46) and Dolphins' Larry Csonka (39) watch.

won the game. Another one was blocked in overtime. The game also marked the last time the Chiefs played at Municipal Stadium. It would be 15 years before the Chiefs returned to the playoffs.

1972

July 29 - Chiefs owner Lamar Hunt is inducted into the Pro Football Hall of Fame in Canton, Ohio.

> *My selection was symbolic of all the general managers, coaches and players who worked for the growth of the American Football League.*
>
> **Lamar Hunt**
> on his Hall of Fame Induction

August 12 - Arrowhead Stadium is dedicated in a pre-season game against the St. Louis Cardinals. The Chiefs win the game, 24-14.

September 17 - In a rematch of the 1971 playoffs, the Chiefs lose to Miami, 20-10, in the first regular season game played at Arrowhead.

October 22 - The winless Eagles embarrass the Chiefs at home, 21-20, the team's third loss without a win at new Arrowhead Stadium.

November 5 - The largest home crowd in Chiefs history, 82,094, jams Arrowhead as the Chiefs beat the Raiders, 27-14.

December 17 - The Chiefs beat the Falcons in Atlanta, 17-14, their third win in a row. It isn't enough though, and the team finishes the season at 8-6 and in second place in the AFC West.

1973

September 16 - The Chiefs lose their season opener for the fourth straight year, falling, 23-13, to the Rams at home.

October 7 - Ed Podolak pulls in a team record 12 receptions as the Chiefs nip Denver at home, 16-14.

October 29 - Kansas City loses at Buffalo, 23-14, on *Monday Night Football.*

November 18 - The Chiefs beat up the Oilers at home, 38-14, and improve their record to 6-3-1.

December 8 - With the Western Division title at stake, the Chiefs go to Oakland and get blown out by the Raiders, 37-7. "It's the worst athletic defeat I've ever suffered," said Ed Podolak after the game.

How do you think I feel? We just got the s--- beat out of us, and you can quote unquote me.

Mike Livingston
after losing to Oakland 37-7

December 16 - Kansas City handily beats the Chargers, 33-6, at Arrowhead, but it's too late. The Chiefs finish the season with a 7-5-2 mark, tied for second in the division.

1974

January 20 - Arrowhead Stadium plays host to the Pro Bowl, a 15-13 win for the AFC. Garo Yepremian booted five fields for the winners.

September 15 - A season-opening win over the Jets, 24-16, at Arrowhead, suggests the Chiefs might still have what it takes to compete for a division title. The coming weeks show they don't.

October 20 -The Chiefs lose a heartbreaker to the Dolphins in Miami, 9-3, dropping the team's record to 2-4.

November 18 - The Chiefs can still perform in prime time, and take a 42-34 victory home from Denver.

December 1 - Hank Stram wins for the last time as the Chiefs head coach. Kansas City defeats the playoff-bound Cardinals in St. Louis, 17-13.

December 14 - The Vikings pound the Chiefs in Minnesota, 35-15, and KC ends the season with a disappointing 5-9 record. It is the club's first losing mark since 1963.

December 27 - Hank Stram is fired. Following the poor 5-9 season, the Chiefs sack the only head coach they've ever had.

Pro football is demanding and changeable, and in the last few weeks I decided that the time had come to revitalize our organization and give it a fresh approach . . . . we are determined that the Chiefs will be a source of pride for the fans in Kansas City and I am confident that the steps taken today will usher in a new era.

Lamar Hunt, 1974
on the firing of Hank Stram

1975

January 23 - Paul Wiggin is named as the Chiefs' new head coach. Wiggin had been an assistant with the 49ers.

Paul Wiggin

September 21 - The Chiefs fall short in the season opener at Denver, 37-33.

October 12 - The 0-3 Chiefs surprise the Raiders at Arrowhead and blow them out, 42-10, Wiggin's first victory as head coach.

November 10 - Monday Night surprise. The Chiefs travel to Dallas and upset the Cowboys on *Monday Night Football*, 34-31.

> *I don't drink champagne but I'm going to have some tonight.*
>
> **Paul Wiggin, 1975**
> after the Chiefs beat the Raiders, 42-10, for his first win

December 7 - Len Dawson plays in his last game for the Chiefs. It's a bad ending though, as the Chargers win at Arrowhead, 28-20. Dawson's season ends when he fractures his right thumb.

December 21 - Oakland takes a little revenge and beats the Chiefs, 28-20, in the final game of the season. Kansas City finishes the year with a 5-9 record.

1976

September 12 - The Chargers come into Arrowhead and spoil the season opener for the Chiefs, winning, 30-16.

September 20 - Kansas City loses a close one at Arrowhead to the Raiders on *Monday Night Football*, 24-21.

October 3 - The Bills thrash the Chiefs in Buffalo, 50-17, the team's fourth straight loss to start the season.

> *I really feel we defeated ourselves.*
>
> **Paul Wiggin, 1976**
> after the Chiefs lost to Buffalo, 50-17

November 7 - The Steelers embarrass the Chiefs at home, 45-0.

December 12 - Kansas City beats the Browns easily, 39-14, and finishes the season with their third straight 5-9 record.

1977

September 18 - A 21-17 loss to the Patriots sets the standard for the rest of the season. The Chiefs don't win a game until October 23.

October 3 - The Raiders play with the Chiefs at Arrowhead, defeating them, 37-28, on *Monday Night Football.*

We're dedicated to seeing the Chiefs competitive with the best teams in the National Football League...There was something missing relating to the performances on the field.

Lamar Hunt
on firing Paul Wiggin

October 31 - Paul Wiggin is fired. Starting the 1977 season 1-6 is too much for Hunt and Steadman. Tom Bettis takes over the head coaching duties for the Chiefs on an interim basis. He coaches the team for the remaining seven games of the season.

I was shocked. I never thought I was doing a bad job.

Paul Wiggin
on being fired

November 6 - Tom Bettis gets his first and only win as head coach when the Chiefs stop the Packers, 20-10.

December 11 - Gary Barbaro returns an interception a team record 102 yards for a touchdown in the Chiefs 34-31 loss to the Seahawks at Arrowhead.

MacArthur Lane

December 18 - Oakland squeaks out a 21-20 win over the Chiefs in the season's final game. The loss leaves KC with a record of 2-12, the worst in the club's history.

December 20 - Marv Levy, who has compiled a successful record as a Canadian Football League coach, is hired as the Chiefs new head coach.

1978

Marv Levy objecting to a call.

September 3 - The Chiefs win the season opener at Cincinnati, 24-23, Marv Levy's first victory as the Chiefs head coach.

October 8 - Tampa Bay comes to Arrowhead and soundly defeats the Chiefs, 30-13.

October 15 - Oakland hands the Chiefs their sixth straight loss, beating them, 28-6.

November 26 - The Chiefs defeat the Chargers, 23-0, for just their third win of the season.

December 17 - Seattle beats the Chiefs, 23-19. Kansas City ends the year with a 4-12 record, finishing last in the AFC West.

1979

Gary Barbaro

September 2 - Kansas City shuts out the Colts at Arrowhead to start the season, 14-0.

September 23 - J.T. Smith returns a punt 88 yards against the Raiders, a franchise record, and the Chiefs cruise to an easy win, 35-7.

September 30 - Chiefs running back Ted McKnight rips off an 84-yard touchdown run, a franchise record, and the Chiefs beat the Seahawks in Seattle, 24-6.

November 4 - Punter Bob Grupp

Henry Marshall and Carlos Carson—top flight receivers.

launches a punt a team record 74 yards in the Chiefs 20-14 loss to San Diego.

December 16 - Fighting the elements more than the Buccaneers, the Chiefs lose to Tampa Bay on a rain swept field, 3-0. Kansas City ends the season with a 7-9 record, last in the AFC West.

1980

Training Camp - Jan Stenerud is released as Nick Lowery wins the placekicker spot on the team. The move is controversial; Lowery has already been cut 11 times by eight different NFL squads.

September 7 - The Chiefs open the season at home and lose to the Raiders, 27-14.

September 14 - Nick Lowery booms a 57-yard field goal in the Chiefs' 17-16 loss to the Seahawks at Arrowhead.

October 5 - In the Raiders rematch, the Chiefs prevail, 31-17. It's the first win of the season and snaps a four-game losing streak.

October 12 - Chiefs quarterback Steve Fuller runs 38 yards for the winning touchdown late in the game as Kansas City sneaks past the Oilers, 21-20.

October 26 - Detroit falls at Arrowhead, 20-17, KC's fourth win in a row.

Art Still

> *It's the first time since I have been coaching here that we have come from behind at the end to win...It was the most excited we have ever been after winning a game.*
>
> **Marv Levy, 1980**
> after the KC beat Oilers, 21-20

December 21 - Kansas City drops the Colts in Baltimore, 38-28, and finishes the season with an 8-8 record. It's the first time since 1973 the Chiefs don't finish the season with a losing record.

1981

September 6 - Kansas City travels to Pittsburgh and brings home a 37-33 victory. The win is a sign of good things to come throughout the season.

October 18 - The Chiefs stop the Broncos at Arrowhead, 28-14. Rookie running back Joe Delaney rips off an 82-yard touchdown run and finishes with 149 rushing yards for the game.

October 25 - Kansas City defeats the Raiders for the second time in three weeks, 28-17. The Chiefs' record improves to 6-2.

November 15 - Joe Delaney rushes for 193 yards against the Oilers at Arrowhead. The Chiefs win, 23-10.

November 26 - Turkey day fiasco. Kansas City loses to Detroit on Thanksgiving, 27-10. It's the beginning of the end for the Chiefs' playoff hopes as their record drops to 8-5.

December 20 - A 10-6 win at Minnesota finishes the season on a high note for the Chiefs. For the first time since 1973 the team has a winning record at the end of the year, a 9-7 mark.

1982

September 12 - Kansas City drops the season opener in Buffalo, 14-9.

September 19 - The Chiefs defeat the Chargers at home, 19-12, to even their record at 1-1. The NFL Players went on strike following the second week of play and wiped out two months of the season.

November 21 - Kansas City loses at New Orleans in their return game from the strike, 27-17.

December 12 - Fourth loss in a row. The Raiders down Kansas City at Arrowhead, 21-16.

Nick Lowery

Joe Delaney, Chiefs rushing standout, met an untimely death in June, 1983.

December 19 - Mile high rout. The Chiefs pound the Broncos, 37-16.

1983

January 2 - The Jets crash at Arrowhead and the Chiefs clean up with a 37-13 win. Only 11,902 fans show up for the season finale of the strike-plagued campaign. KC finishes with a 3-6 record.

January 4 - Marv Levy takes the fall for the Chiefs' poor season and is fired.

> *The only emotion I felt was disappointment. There is not bitterness, no animosity.*
>
> **Marv Levy**
> on being fired

February 3 - John Mackovic is chosen as the Chiefs new head coach. Club President Jack Steadman said, "He's one of the brightest young men I have ever met at any age. I had tremendous recommendation on him."

June 29 - Joe Delaney, the Chiefs' young superstar running back, drowns while trying to rescue three children from a park pond in Monroe, Louisiana. Only 24, Delaney promised to become one of the franchise's greatest runners.

> *He had all the qualities and character traits that you look up to in great people. Courage, tenacity, honesty, loyalty.*
>
> **Tom Condon**
> on Joe Delaney

July 30 - Bobby Bell becomes the first Chiefs player inducted into the Pro Football Hall of Fame in Canton, Ohio.

September 18 - Nick Lowery booms a club-record 58-yard field goal for the Chiefs in Washington against the Redskins. Kansas City loses the game, 27-12.

December 11 - Bill Kenney completes 31 of 41 passes for 411 yards and four touchdowns against the Chargers in San Diego. The effort falls short however, as the Chiefs lose, 41-38.

December 18 - Nobody loves losers. Before the meager crowd of 11,377 spectators at Arrowhead, the Chiefs end the season by thumping the playoff-bound Broncos, 48-17. Kansas City finishes at 6-10 and ties for fourth in the division.

1984

September 2 - Kansas City opens at Pittsburgh and defeats the Steelers, 37-27.

October 14 - Wide receiver Carlos Carson catches seven passes for 165 yards in the Chiefs' 31-13 win over the Chargers.

November 4 - Seattle routs the Chiefs in the Kingdome, 45-0.

December 9 - Payback. The Chiefs easily gain revenge on the Seahawks and beat them at Arrowhead, 34-7.

December 16 - An easy win over San Diego, 42-21, closes out the season for Kansas City. The Chiefs finish with a respectable record of 8-8.

1985

September 8 - Bill Kenney passes for 397 yards and three touchdowns as the Chiefs smother the Saints in New Orleans, 47-27.

September 12 - Nick Lowery kicks the second 58-yard field goal of his career as the Chiefs whip the Raiders at home, 36-20.

September 29 - Chiefs free safety Deron Cherry ties an NFL record with four interceptions against the Seahawks at Arrowhead, and KC wins, 28-7.

Stephone Paige

November 17 - The Chiefs lose to the 49ers, 31-3, their seventh loss in a row.

December 22 - Wide receiver Stephone Paige has eight receptions and racks up 309 receiving yards, a then-NFL record, as the Chiefs close out the season by beating San Diego, 38-34. The team still finishes in last place with a 6-10 record.

1986

August 2 - Chiefs great middle linebacker, Willie Lanier, is inducted into the Pro Football Hall of Fame in Canton, Ohio.

Bill Kenney

September 7 - Kansas City starts the season with a 24-14 win over the Bengals at Arrowhead.

October 19 - The Chiefs squeak out a win over the Chargers at home, 42-41. The victory improves the team's record to 4-3.

November 9 - Seattle comes to Arrowhead and goes home a loser. The Chiefs win a relatively easy game, 27-7. After 10 games, Kansas City's record is 7-3.

November 30 - The Chiefs appear to be out of the playoff hunt when they drop their third game in a row, losing to Buffalo at home, 17-14.

> *We had a monkey the size of King Kong on our backs. He's off our backs now, and it's time to start writing our own history.*
>
> **Nick Lowery**
> after Chiefs clinch
> 1986 playoff spot

December 14 - The Chiefs sneak by the Raiders in Los Angeles, 20-17.

December 21 - Back to the playoffs. After a 15-year absence, the Chiefs return to post-season play by beating the Steelers in Pittsburgh, 24-19. All of Kansas City's points came by way of the special teams, and despite giving up more than 500 yards of offense to the Steelers, the Chiefs hang on and win.

December 28 - AFC Wildcard Playoff game. The Chiefs travel to New York for their first playoff game in 15 years. They make an early exit, losing to the Jets, 35-15.

Dino Hackett

KC took an early 6-0 lead on Jeff Smith's one-yard touchdown run, but the Jets scored 28 straight points to put the game away by the fourth quarter.

1987

January 8 - Despite leading the Chiefs into the playoffs for the first time in 15 years, John Mackovic is fired. The move leaves a lot of people perplexed.

> *Competitive greatness means winning the big games, the games on the road in the division, the playoff games ... There's a very strong feeling ... that we can move in that direction.*
>
> **Frank Gansz**

January 10 - Frank Gansz, special teams coach under Mackovic, is named head coach of the Chiefs.

Frank Gansz

August 8 - Chiefs quarterback, Len Dawson, is inducted into the Pro Football Hall of Fame in Canton, Ohio.

September 13 - The Chiefs win the season opener at Arrowhead against the Chargers, 20-13. Two rookies, Paul Palmer and Christian Okoye, star in the win. Palmer returns a kickoff for a touchdown and Okoye rushes for 105 yards.

September 27 - Because of the players strike, the Chiefs game with the Vikings is cancelled. All NFL teams put together "replacement" teams to continue playing.

October 18 - The Chiefs replacement team loses its third straight game, this time to Denver, 26-17. The team's record is now 1-4, a hole the regulars are unable to recover from.

October 25 - So much for the regulars. San Diego easily beats the "real" Chiefs in their return game from the strike, 42-21. Carlos Carson stars for KC and accumulates 197 receiving yards.

November 22 - Green Bay travels to Arrowhead and wins, 23-3. It's the Chiefs team-record ninth loss in a row.

December 27 - Another disastrous strike season — at least for the Chiefs — ends. KC beats Seattle, 41-20, to end with a 4-11 record and another last place finish.

1988

March 31 - The Chiefs send safety Mark Robinson and two 1988 draft picks (fourth and eighth rounds) to Tampa Bay for quarterback Steve DeBerg.

September 4 - Kansas City starts the season with a loss at home to Cleveland, 6-3.

September 18 - The Chiefs beat the Broncos at Arrowhead, 20-13.

November 13 - With their 31-28 win over the Bengals, the Chiefs stop their seven-game no-win streak.

December 18 - The Chiefs lose at San Diego, 24-13, and finish the season with a record of 4-11-1 — last in the AFC West.

December 19 - Carl Peterson is named President/General Manager/CEO of the Chiefs.

Christian Okoye

1989

January 5 - Carl Peterson fires Frank Gansz.

January 24 - Marty Schottenheimer becomes the Chiefs head coach. He is the first head coach hired by the Chiefs who has experience as a head coach in the NFL (Cleveland).

March 30 - Nine-time pro bowler Mike Webster, who originally joined the Chiefs in February as a line coach, decides to play again.

> *My coaching philosophy is quite simple. The best way to establish a position of excellence in the National Football League is first to expect it. I've always felt the worst thing you can ever do is arbitrarily set a goal that might well be beneath what you are capable of achieving.*
>
> **Marty Schottenheimer**
> after being named the
> Chiefs head coach

Steve DeBerg

September 10 - The Schottenheimer era starts with a loss at Denver, 34-20.

September 17 - Marty gets his first Chiefs win against the Raiders as Kansas City downs the silver and black at Arrowhead, 24-19.

October 22 - Christian Okoye carries the ball 33 times and racks up 170 rushing yards as the Chiefs defeat the Cowboys at Arrowhead, 36-28.

November 26 - Kansas City throws a whitewash on the Oilers, 34-0.

December 24 - The Chiefs defeat the Dolphins for the second time, 27-24, but still miss the playoffs. They do finish with a winning record, 8-7-1, providing optimism for the immediate future.

1990

August 4 - Buck Buchanan, Chiefs defensive tackle, is inducted into the Pro Football Hall of Fame in Canton, Ohio.

September 17 - Stephone Paige pulls in ten pass receptions for 206 yards, but the Chiefs still come up short in Denver, 24-23, on *Monday Night Football*.

Derrick Thomas

Barry Word

October 14 - Barry Word rushes for a team record 200 yards against Detroit at Arrowhead. The Chiefs smother the Lions, 43-24.

November 11 - Derrick Thomas sacks Seattle quarterback Dave Krieg an NFL record seven times, but it's not enough. On the game's last play, Krieg eludes Thomas and throws a game-winning touchdown pass. The Seahawks win at Arrowhead, 17-16.

December 9 - Playoff bound. Kansas City beats the Broncos, 31-20, and clinches a spot in the playoffs.

December 29 - The Chiefs close out the regular season with a 21-10 win at Chicago. KC finishes with an 11-5 mark, the club's best since 1969. Free-agent running back Barry Word rushes for 1,015 yards and quarterback Steve DeBerg finishes out a career year, tossing 23 touchdown passes while ringing up 3,444 yards in the air. The Chiefs make the playoffs as a Wild Card entry.

1991

> *It's tough to have the year end this way.*
>
> **Steve DeBerg**
> after the loss to Miami
> in the 1990 playoff game

January 5 - The Chiefs suffer a heart-wrenching loss to the Dolphins, 17-16, in the AFC Wild Card game. Leading 16-3 in the fourth quarter, KC gave up two touchdowns, but were driving for a game-winning score when a questionable holding call brought back a long run by Okoye. Lowery's 52-yard field goal attempt fell short, and so did the Chiefs.

July 27 - Jan Stenerud is inducted into the Pro Football Hall of Fame in Canton, Ohio.

September 1 - Kansas City clips the Falcons' wings in the season opener at Arrowhead, 14-3.

September 16 - Houston stops the Chiefs on *Monday Night Football*, 17-7.

October 7 - The Chiefs trounce the Bills at Arrowhead on *Monday Night Football*, 33-6. It's the Chiefs first home *Monday Night Football* game in eight years.

Neil Smith

October 13 - Miami comes to Arrowhead and is lucky to leave alive. The Chiefs toy with the Dolphins and win easily, 42-7. Okoye runs for 153 yards.

October 28 - Kansas City comes from behind on *Monday Night Football* and beats the Raiders, 24-21. The win puts the team's record at 6-3.

November 24 - A tough loss at Cleveland. Kansas City loses to the Browns, 20-15, which leaves a tough road to the playoffs.

December 22 - In a strange twist of playoff circumstances, the Chiefs meet the Raiders on the season's final Sunday. The winner will have home-field advantage when the two rivals meet again the following week in the first round of the AFC playoffs. Kansas City prevails, winning a hard-fought game, 27-21. J.J. Birden stars for KC, catching 8 passes for 188 yards. The Chiefs' close the regular season at 10-6.

Dan Saleaumua

December 28 - Playoff success. The Chiefs win their first post-season game since Super Bowl IV, edging the Raiders, 10-6, in the first-ever playoff game at Arrowhead Stadium. The Chiefs' defense forces six Raider turnovers.

1992

January 5 - Buffaloed. The Bills have too much offensive punch and take an easy win from the Chiefs in the second round of the playoffs, 37-14.

July 16 - Chiefs great and Hall-of-Famer Buck Buchanan loses his battle with cancer and passes away.

September 6 - Kansas City travels to San Diego and beats the Chargers on opening day, 24-10.

September 28 - Another successful *Monday Night Football* game for Kansas City. The Raiders come to Arrowhead and lose to the Chiefs for the sixth straight time, 27-7.

October 25 - The Chiefs are easily handled by the Steelers at Arrowhead, 27-3. The loss leaves Kansas City's record at 4-4.

November 29 - The Jets fall to Kansas City at Shea Stadium, 23-7. It's the Chiefs' fourth win in a row and thrusts them back into the playoff picture.

December 6 - After six losses in a row to the Chiefs, the Raiders finally beat KC, 28-7, at Los Angeles.

December 27 - With the season and a playoff berth on the line for the team that wins, the Chiefs rise to the occasion and bury the Broncos at Arrowhead, 42-20, sending Denver home for the year. The Chiefs finish at 10-6, and will play at San Diego in the first round of the playoffs.

1993

January 2 - Kansas City exits quickly and quietly from playoffs, losing to the Chargers, 17-0, in San Diego.

April 20 - Super Joe comes to Kansas City. The Chiefs trade a first round pick in the 1993 draft to the San Francisco 49ers for Joe Montana. KC also gets safety David Whitmore and a third-round pick in the trade.

June 9 - Marcus Allen signs with the Chiefs. The future Hall-of-Fame running back signs a multi-year deal with Kansas City.

> *I am not going to put any pressure on Joe Montana that he has to work miracles. Our hope is that he can help us take another step in regards to the improvement of the Kansas City Chiefs.*
>
> **Carl Peterson**
> on signing Joe Montana

> *This is the one guy Marty Schottenheimer wanted from the first day of free-agency.*
>
> **Carl Peterson**
> on signing Marcus Allen

Joe Montana and Marcus Allen

September 5 - The Montana-Allen era of Kansas City football begins with a 27-3 win over the hapless Tampa Bay Bucs. Montana passes for 246 yards and three touchdowns in his debut, but hurts his wrist and misses the next game.

September 20 - Denver visits Arrowhead on *Monday Night Football*. The Chiefs sputter up and down the field, but prevail, 15-7, on the strength of five Nick Lowery field goals.

October 3 - Marcus Allen scores the 100th touchdown of his career against his former team, the Raiders. The Chiefs take the game from the Raiders, 24-9.

October 17 - A close game with the Chargers. Kansas City nips San Diego, 17-14, improving their record to 5-1.

October 31 - No treats, nothing but tricks. The Dolphins bring the Chiefs back to earth a little, easily beating them in Miami, 30-10.

November 21 - Without Montana, the Chiefs play poorly and lose to Chicago at home, 19-17.

November 28 - Buffalo stew. The Chiefs cut up the defending AFC champs at Arrowhead, 23-7. Montana has two touchdown passes in the game.

December 19 - Montana tosses a couple of touchdown passes and the Chiefs, after being down, 17-0, come back and beat the Chargers at home, 28-24.

When all is said and done and Joe finishes his career as a player in three or four years, they'll talk about him as one of the greatest quarterbacks in history.

Marty Schottenheimer
on Joe Montana after 1993 playoff game with Pittsburgh

December 26 - The Vikings embarrass the Chiefs in Minnesota, 30-10. The loss prevents Kansas City from having home field advantage in the playoffs.

1994

January 2 - Western Division Champs. Todd McNair runs for a pair of touchdowns as the Chiefs win their first division title since 1971 by defeating the Seahawks, 34-24. Kansas City finishes the regular season at

Ricky Siglar (66), Keith Cash (89) and Joe Montana celebrate Cash's seven-yard touchdown reception the 1993 Divisional Playoff against the Oilers.

11-5. Joe Montana, Marcus Allen, John Alt, Neil Smith and Derrick Thomas make the Pro Bowl.

Joe Phillips sacks the Oilers' Warren Moon in the 1993 Divisional Playoff game.

January 8 - Montana Magic at its best! A fourth-down touchdown pass from Montana ties the game with 46 seconds left. Lowery hits a 32-yard field in overtime, and the Chiefs beat the Steelers at Arrowhead, 27-24, and take the AFC first round playoff game.

January 16 - The Chiefs topple heavily-favored Houston in the Astrodome, 28-20, and advance to the AFC Championship for the first time ever. Montana performs brilliantly in the fourth quarter, hitting two of his three touchdown passes in the game. Allen scores on a 21-yard run late to seal the win and send the Chiefs to Buffalo for the conference title game.

January 23 - The Super Bowl dream dies. The Chiefs playoff run ends as Buffalo wins their fourth straight AFC Championship, downing Kansas City, 30-13. Montana suffers a concussion in the third quarter and the Chiefs were never able to mount a serious threat after that to get back in the game.

April 6 - The Chiefs sign kicker Lin Elliott to replace Nick Lowery, who left Kansas City for the Jets.

Derrick Thomas sacks 49ers quarterback Steve Young.

September 4 - The Chiefs open the 1994 season with a 30-17 win at New Orleans.

September 11 - Facing his former teammates, Montana leads the Chiefs to a 24-17 win over the 49ers at Arrowhead.

September 25 - The Rams come to Arrowhead and shock the Chiefs, 16-0.

October 17 - *Monday Night* comeback. Montana leads the Chiefs to a dramatic win over the Broncos on *Monday Night Football.* Joe hit 34 of 54 pass attempts for 393 yards and three touchdowns, the last one to J.J. Birden for the winning score. The win improved the Chiefs record to 4-2.

November 20 - The Chiefs drop Cleveland at Arrowhead, 20-13, improving their record to 7-4.

December 24 - Marcus Allen gains 132 yards rushing as the Chiefs beat the Raiders in Los Angeles, 19-9. The win secured a playoff spot for the Chiefs, their fifth straight. Kansas City finishes with a 9-7 record.

December 31 - The playoff experience was short-lived for the Chiefs as they lose, 27-17, to the Dolphins in Miami.

1995

April - The Chiefs sign free agent quarterback Rich Gannon.

April 19 - Joe Montana announces his retirement at a morning news conference.

September 3 - Kansas City opens the season with a convincing 34-10 win over the Seahawks in Seattle.

September 10 - The Chiefs score two touchdowns in the fourth quarter and then take the Giants in overtime, 20-17. The win sets up several exciting finishes for the Chiefs throughout the season.

September 17 - More overtime magic. James Hasty picks off a Jeff Hostetler pass and returns it for a touchdown in overtime as the Chiefs beat the Raiders again, 23-17.

Tamarick Vanover

October 1 - The Cardinals are easy prey for the Chiefs. Chiefs quarterback Steve Bono tosses two touchdown passes and rambles 76 yards for another score as Kansas City beats Arizona, 24-3.

October 9 - Tamarick Vanover returns a punt 86 yards in overtime to give the Chiefs a 29-23 victory over San Diego on *Monday Night Football.* It is the Chiefs' third overtime win at home during the 1995 season.

October 22 - For the second year in a row, the Chiefs go to Mile High Stadium and beat the Broncos, 21-7.

November 19 - The Chiefs win their seventh game in a row, beating the Oilers at home, 20-13.

November 23 - Dallas stops the Chiefs on Thanksgiving, 24-12.

December 24 - Tamarick Vanover runs the opening kickoff 89 yards for a touchdown and the Chiefs never look back as they clinch home-field advantage throughout the playoffs. The AFC Western Division champs finish the regular season with a 13-3 record, the best in the NFL. Greg Hill leads Kansas City with 113 yards rushing.

Dale Carter

1996

January 7 - Oh, what might have been. In bitter cold conditions, the Chiefs fail on all accounts and suffer a disastrous upset loss to the Indianapolis Colts at Arrowhead Stadium, 10-7, and make an early, embarrassing exit from the playoffs. Lin Elliott missed a 42-yard field goal attempt in the final seconds of the game — his third failure of the day — that would have tied the score. Steve Bono threw three interceptions and was replaced late in the game by Rich Gannon. Marcus Allen gained 94 yards rushing for the Chiefs in the losing effort.

Once you get into the playoffs, everything you've done in the regular season is gone. The slate is clean. Right now, I feel like we didn't accomplish anything. The disappointment makes it feel that way.

Steve Bono
after losing to the Colts in 1995 Divisional Playoff game

You can't tell by the result, but I felt like I was going to get the job done.

Lin Elliott
on missing his third field goal against the Colts

Lin Elliott kicks and then watches with holder Louie Aguiar as his game-tying field goal attempt misses in the waning seconds of the 1995 Divisional Playoff game with the Colts. It is his third miss of the game. The Chiefs lost, 10-7.

August 21 - Kicker Pete Stoyanovich comes to Kansas City from Miami for a fifth-round draft pick. Stoyanovich replaces Lin Elliott, who was released by the Chiefs earlier in the year.

Steve Bono

September 1 - The Chiefs hang on and win the season opener at Houston, 20-19.

September 22 - The Broncos fall short and Kansas City beats them, 17-14, the fourth win in a row for the Chiefs.

October 7 - Pittsburgh comes to Arrowhead on *Monday Night Football* and runs over the Chiefs, 17-7.

November 17 - Kansas City holds off the Bears and wins, 14-10, improving their record to 8-3.

November 28 - Another Thanksgiving Day game, and this time KC wins at Detroit, 28-24.

December 9 - The beginning of the end of KC's playoff run. The Raiders plow through the Chiefs and beat them handily on *Monday Night Football*, 26-7.

December 15 - The Colts come into Arrowhead and upset the Chiefs again, 24-19.

December 22 - Kansas City travels to Buffalo and plays miserably, losing to the Bills, 20-9. It's the team's third loss in a row and drops them out of the playoffs, the first time they miss the post-season party since 1989.

1997

March 17 - Free agent quarterback Elvis Grbac signs with the Chiefs.

April 14 - Free agent Neil Smith leaves KC and signs with the Broncos.

June 18 - Wide Receiver Andre Rison signs with the Chiefs.

August 31 - The Chiefs open in Denver and give a lackluster performance as they lose to the Broncos, 19-3.

Andre Rison

September 8 - *Monday Night Football* comeback. Elvis Grbac hits Andre Rison with three seconds left to lead the Chiefs to an improbable comeback win over the Raiders in Oakland, 28-27. The win ignites the Chiefs for the rest of the season.

> *I couldn't believe we got in the end zone. They had all those defensive backs out there. They rushed only three defensive linemen.*
>
> **David Szott**
> on KC's last-second, game-winning touchdown against the Raiders

September 28 - A shaky performance by Kansas City, but a win nonetheless. Elvis Grbac throws three interceptions, but the Chiefs are able to overcome a 10-point deficit and defeat Seattle in overtime, 20-17.

Elvis Grbac

October 5 - The Chiefs again fail to defeat an inferior Dolphin team in Miami and lose, 17-14. KC manages only 96 yards rushing and 177 yards passing.

October 7 - Kansas City sends a fifth-round draft pick to the Packers for linebacker Wayne Simmons, a move which greatly bolsters the Chiefs' defense for the rest of the season.

October 16 - Grbac tosses two touchdown passes as the Chiefs down the Chargers, 31-3, at Arrowhead.

November 3 - After falling behind, 10-0, the Chiefs battle back and win a hard-fought *Monday Night Football* game with the Steelers, 13-10. The victory has its price though—Grbac goes down with a fractured clavicle and misses the next six games.

November 9 - A sloppy performance leads to a bad loss. Rich Gannon steps in for the injured Grbac and takes a beating from the Jacksonville Jaguars, who record six sacks. Two interceptions and three lost fumbles contribute to the Chiefs 24-10 defeat. The Chiefs will not lose again during the regular season.

Pete Stoyanovich

November 16 - Big, big win. After falling behind, 13-0, the Chiefs regroup, and playing with a minimum number of mistakes, surprise the Broncos at Arrowhead. Pete Stoyanovich launched a 54-yard line-drive field goal as time expired and the Chiefs beat the Broncos, 24-22.

Rich Gannon

Derrick Thomas recorded his 100th career sack during the game, downing Denver's John Elway for the honor. Marcus Allen scored two touchdowns.

November 30 - The Chiefs absolutely destroy the 49ers, romping to an incredibly easy win at Arrowhead, 44-9. Gannon throws three touchdown passes, Allen scores a touchdown and passes for another, and the defense records five sacks in the dominating performance. KC's record improves to 10-3.

December 7 - Raider-hater delight. Oakland comes to Arrowhead and does nothing. The Chiefs hammer their top-rival, 30-0. The KC defense holds Oakland to a meager 93 total yards on offense. Stoyonovich kicks three field goals, Donnell Bennett and Gannon rush for touchdowns, and the defense racks up five sacks.

December 21 - Division Champs. For the second time in three years, the Chiefs win the AFC West with their 25-13 win over the New Orleans Saints at Arrowhead. The team clinched the home field throughout the playoffs the week before. Kansas City finishes with a 13-3 record and was undefeated on Arrowhead's turf.

1998

January 4 - There was no comeback, no last-second pass completion, no defensive stand protecting a lead. With the fruits and rewards of their outstanding season on the line, the Chiefs fail to convert on a last-ditch drive and lose to the Denver Broncos at Arrowhead, 14-10, ending their season and once again leaving the team, coaches and city to ponder an incredible number of "what-ifs" for the rest of the winter. The Chiefs held the Broncos to 272 yards total offense and committed no turnovers, and *still* couldn't control the action. A bad call in the end zone, a missed

Tight end Tony Gonzalez celebrates after scoring the Chiefs' only touchdown in the 1997 playoff against Denver.

field goal and a poorly-timed fake field goal attempt cost the Chiefs. In the final seconds of the game, Elvis Grbac's fourth down pass to Lake Dawson fell incomplete and the Broncos moved on to the AFC title game. The Chiefs were left with only one task — cleaning out their lockers.

> *I will not feel sorry for myself. I do not believe in self-pity. And I have such a distaste for people who do. I think it's wrong. I really do.*
>
> **Marty Schottenheimer**
> after losing 1997 Divisional Playoff to Denver

March 2 - Wide receiver Derrick Alexander, an unrestricted free agent, signs with the Chiefs.

April 9 - Marcus Allen announces his retirement.

April 17 - The Chiefs sign free-agent defensive end Leslie O'Neal.

April 18 - The Chiefs sign free-agent defensive end Chester McGlockton.

September 6 - The Chiefs open the 1998 season with an impressive display of defensive muscle and easily defeat the Raiders at Arrowhead, 28-8. Kansas City sacks the Raiders' quarterbacks 10 times, with Derrick Thomas racking up six by himself. Donnell Bennett rushes for 115 yards and a touchdown to lead the offense, but Elvis Grbac suffers a sprained shoulder and misses the next four games.

September 13 - The offense is sluggish and inconsistent as Kansas City falls to Jacksonville, 21-16. Rich Gannon, taking over for the injured Grbac, throws for 263 yards, but the Chiefs can't get into the end zone until less than five minutes remain in the game.

October 4 - Kansas City conquers the Seahawks and the rain at Arrowhead, 17-6. Gannon hit Andre Rison for an 80-yard touchdown pass after a 54-minute rain delay caused by a violent storm. The two teams combined for nine turnovers, five by KC. The win puts the Chiefs' record at 4-1.

October 11 - The Chiefs are humiliated by the Patriots at Foxboro Stadium, 40-10. Grbac returns, but does little for the ineffective offense.

October 13 - To bolster their sagging running game, the Chiefs trade a fifth round draft pick to the Chicago Bears for Bam Morris, a running back best known for checkered past.

Bam Morris

November 1 - In another driving rainstorm, Grbac throws three interceptions and the Chiefs blow the game against the Jets, losing 20-17.

November 16 - The Chiefs put on one of the worst displays of disgraceful sportsmanship in the franchise's history as they are easily beaten by the Broncos at Arrowhead on *Monday Night Football*, 30-7. Kansas City is flagged for five personal foul penalties — three by Derrick Thomas — during the Broncos' final touchdown drive. "I could not in my worst nightmare imagine the conduct that took place at the end of the game," said Schottenheimer afterwards.

> *I allowed my situation to get out of hand. My actions of (Monday) will never occur again. Being one of the individuals everybody looks up to on this football team, I have to conduct myself in a positive manner at all times.*
>
> **Derrick Thomas**
> during his apology for his behavior in the Denver game

November 17 - Fallout continues from the Denver game. The Chiefs release linebacker Wayne Simmons and suspend Derrick Thomas for one game.

> *I don't think that there's any question that losing leads to losing like winning leads to winning.*
>
> **Marty Schottenheimer**
> after the Chiefs' sixth loss in a row

November 22 - San Diego scores 21 fourth quarter points and sneaks past the Chiefs, 38-37. It's Kansas City's sixth loss on a row, the team's longest losing streak since they dropped nine in a row in 1987. Bam Morris scores three touchdowns and Stoyanovich boots a 50-yard field goal in the losing effort. The Chiefs' record stands at 4-7.

Tim Grunhard

November 29 - Kansas City snaps the losing streak against the Arizona Cardinals at Arrowhead, winning 34-24. "There's a lot of fight in this team," said Gannon, who tossed three touchdown passes in the game. "It's nice to get the win."

December 13 - Bam Morris runs through the Dallas Cowboys defense for 137 yards and a touchdown to lead the Chiefs to a 20-17 win at Arrowhead. " Marty told us we were going to run the ball this week and the line did a great job," Morris said after game. The win was Schottenheimer's 100th as the Chiefs head coach.

December 20 - The Chiefs play a flat, uninspired game at New York and lose to the Giants, 28-7. Gannon and Grbac throw two interceptions each, and the team rushes for only 66 yards. "It didn't start out well and it just kind of snowballed from there," said Gannon. "It just seemed like we couldn't get anything going."

December 26 - After trailing 14-0, the Chiefs come back and surprise the Raiders in Oakland, 31-24. Grbac hit Tony Gonzalez with the game-winning touchdown late in the fourth quarter. Morris runs for 96 yards and two touchdowns. The win leaves the Chiefs record at 7-9, fourth in the AFC West. It's the worst record in Schottenheimer's coaching career.

> *Because it was the Raiders, we were able to come back. Because it's Jeff George, our spirits picked up.*
>
> **Elvis Grbac**
> after the Chiefs beat the Raiders to end the '98 season

1999

January 11 - Marty Schottenheimer resigns as head coach of the Chiefs. His career record with Kansas City was 101-58-1, which produced the best winning percentage in the club's history (.631). But his playoff record with the Chiefs was a miserable 3-7. The 1998 season was the first time Schottenheimer finished a season with a losing mark. "It was a golden era of Chiefs football," Lamar Hunt said of Schottenheimer's tenure as head coach.

> *It's been a heck of a good ride. Maybe the individual that Lamar (Hunt) and Carl (Peterson) hires will have the opportunity to fulfill the things that we were unable to do.*
>
> **Marty Schottenheimer**
> at the press conference announcing his retirement

January 22 - After looking at several candidates, Carl Peterson chooses Chiefs defensive coordinator Gunther Cunningham as the team's new head coach, and a new era of Chiefs football begins. Cunningham has been with the team four years and has never been a head coach in the NFL. "I interviewed a lot of talented people," said Peterson, "but throughout the process, I kept coming back to Gunther Cunningham."

February 12 - After sitting out the 1998 season because of contract negotiation problems, Chiefs defensive end Dan Williams agrees to terms and signs a six-year contract.

Carl Peterson and Gunther Cunningham share a happy moment at the press conference announcing Cunningham as the Chiefs' new head coach.

February 13 - Rich Gannon leaves the Chiefs and signs with the Raiders.

February 16 - Dale Carter leaves Kansas City and signs with the Broncos.

February 18 - The Chiefs sign cornerback Carlton Gray, a free agent from the New York Giants, to a five-year contract.

> *I am euphoric at finally getting the opportunity to do this. I have sat through meeting after meeting after meeting and learned and learned and I am ready to put my mark on a football team. I know exactly what to do.*
>
> **Gunther Cunningham**
> on being the Chiefs
> new head coach

April 26 - Warren Moon signs a two-year deal with the Chiefs. The prolific passer is expected to be Grbac's backup.

April 27 - The Chiefs sign free agent linebacker Marvcus Patton.

May 13 - Free agent cornerback Chris Dishman signs a three-year deal with the Chiefs.

August 15 - The Gunther Cunningham era begins with a pre-season victory over the Tennessee Titans at Arrowhead, 22-20.

> *Warren gives us the veteran quarterback experience that every team would like to have. His experience and leadership on the field, in the classroom and in the locker room will be similar to that which Marcus Allen brought us.*
>
> **Carl Peterson**
> on signing Warren Moon

Warren Moon

Chiefs Players Trivia

Len Dawson

Len Dawson

(1962-75)

Len Dawson was the quiet assassin. He could say more with a stare than most players could with words. He was the team leader, no doubt about it.

Ed Podolak
on Len Dawson

After riding the bench for five disappointing seasons in the NFL, Len Dawson went to Dallas hoping to resurrect his football career with the Texans of the AFL. It was a good move. Twenty-five years later he arrived in Canton, Ohio, and took his place among the greats of the game at the Pro Football Hall of Fame. His brilliant play and leadership guided the franchise to three league championships and a world championship.

Hank Stram referred to his star quarterback as "the most accurate passer in pro football." But "Lenny the Cool," a nickname he earned for always remaining calm in the toughest of game situations, was also one of the best leaders. Dawson rode through a rough storm before Super Bowl IV when he was wrongly accused of gambling. He responded with an MVP performance against the Vikings, and secured his place as the Chiefs greatest signal caller of all-time.

1. Where was Dawson born?

2. Was Dawson an All-American at Purdue?

3. What two NFL teams did Dawson play for before joining the Dallas Texans?

4. What round of the NFL draft was Dawson drafted?

5. How many times did Dawson win the AFL passing title?

6. Dawson holds the Chiefs career mark for pass rating. What is it?

7. How many touchdown passes did he throw in his career?

8. How many of those touchdown passes were with the Chiefs/Texans?

9. How many times did he lead the league in touchdown passes?

10. What's the most touchdown passes he had in a single season?

11. How many rushing touchdowns did he have in his career?

12. What's the highest total of yards he threw for in a single season?

13. How many yards passing did have in his career?

14. Dawson lead the AFL and NFL combined in completion percentage eight times. What years did he do it?

15. How many times was he named to the AFL All-Star game and Pro Bowl?

16. Dawson was named AFL Player of the Year once. What year did he win the award?

17. In addition to his TV and radio commitments in Kansas City, what national TV show does Dawson co-host every week during the NFL season?

Marcus Allen

(1993-97)

The atmosphere in Kansas City was remarkable. I immediately sensed a single-minded determination among the players and coaches to do whatever was necessary to become an outstanding team. And the fan support was unbelievable.

Marcus Allen
on coming to the Chiefs

Given up for dead by the Raiders, Marcus Allen came to Kansas City and not only revived his career, but flourished. He was also a big part of the Chiefs' success, leading the team to the playoffs four of the five seasons he played for Kansas City.

Marcus meant victories. He scored more touchdowns rushing during his tenure with the Chiefs than any back in Kansas City had before him. He was incredibly consistent when it came to gaining first downs or touchdowns in short yardage situations, and his blocking skills, unselfish play and leadership qualities were a big reason why the Chiefs won 55 games with him on the field.

1. Where did Allen attend high school?

2. Two other running backs were chosen before him in the 1982 NFL draft. Who were they?

3. When Allen was a member of the Raiders, what was their record against the Chiefs?

4. When he was a member of the Chiefs, what was their record against the Raiders?

5. What's the most yards rushing Allen gained in a regular season game?

6. What's the most yards rushing Allen gained in a post-season game?

7. What's the most yards rushing Allen gained in a regular season game with the Chiefs?

Marcus Allen

8. What's the most yards rushing Allen gained in a playoff game with the Chiefs?

9. Going into the 1998 season, Allen was the NFL's all-time leader in rushing touchdowns. How many does he have?

10. How many of those rushing touchdowns were with the Chiefs?

11. How many total touchdowns does he have?

12. Allen threw three passes for the Chiefs. How many were for touchdowns?

13. How many 100-yard rushing games did Allen have for the Chiefs?

14. How many times was Allen selected for the Pro Bowl as a Chief?

15. Allen was second on the Chiefs in rushing yards in 1997. Who was first?

16. At the start of the 1998 season, Allen was the NFL record holder for most games played by a running back. How many games had he played in?

17. He is also the record holder for most pass receptions by a running back. How many does he have?

18. At the start of the 1998 season, Allen was second in career rushing attempts. Who is first?

Bobby Bell

(1963-74)

Bobby Bell is the greatest outside linebacker who ever played the game ... He is the only player I have seen who could play any position on a team and that team could still win.

Hank Stram
at Bell's Hall of Fame induction

When Bobby Bell came to the Chiefs from college, it is not a stretch to say he could have played any position on the team and not only excelled, but been an all-star. He could throw a football the length of the field, outrun most fullbacks and punt with the best kickers in the league. He was truly an all-around football player, a great athlete.

And he became one of the greatest outside linebackers of all time.

Bell's dominating play helped lead the Chiefs to two Super Bowls and a World Championship in 1969. Of the numerous honors, awards and achievements he accumulated throughout his career and after, the fact Bell was the first Chief inducted into Pro Football's Hall of Fame says the most for his extraordinary talent. Bell was also named to the All-Time AFL team.

1. Where did Bell go to high school?
2. What position did he play in high school?
3. Where did Bell go to college?
4. What prestigious football award did Bell win after his senior year?
5. In which round was Bell drafted by the Chiefs?
6. Was he drafted by an NFL team? If so, which one?
7. What position did he first play for Kansas City?
8. How many times was he selected for the All-AFL/All-AFC team?

Bobby Bell

Willie Lanier

Willie Lanier

(1967-77)

His destiny was to be the prototype middle linebacker of his era.

Lamar Hunt
at Lanier's Hall of Fame induction

His tackling style was so ferocious, thunderous and aggressive, his hits had a sound all their own. In addition to his tackling, he had the other ingredients of greatness—speed, savvy, durability and size. He was always the key to the Chiefs' great defenses.

But he was more than just a hitter; his leadership qualities were just as important to the Chiefs. Willie's inspired play and pleadings led the Chiefs in the greatest goal-line stand in the club's history during the 1969 AFL Divisional playoff with the Jets. After holding New York to a field goal, the Chiefs won the game and, ultimately, the Super Bowl.

Lanier was inducted into the Pro Football Hall of Fame in 1986.

1. Where did Lanier go to college?
2. Lanier was named MVP of what college bowl game?
3. What round of the draft was Lanier selected by the Chiefs?
4. How many AFL All-Star games and Pro Bowls did Lanier play in?
5. How many career interceptions did he have?
6. What was his highest single-season interception total?
7. How many career fumble recoveries does he have?
8. Lanier had two different nicknames. What were they?
9. How many touchdowns did he score in his career?

Derrick Thomas

(1989-99)

It's a mind-set. You are going to get double-teamed, triple-teamed and you just have to do something to offset what they are doing to you and to keep going and never stop.

Derrick Thomas
on rushing the passer

Derrick Thomas is one of the most dominant players in the Chiefs' illustrious defensive tradition. He is a linebacker who wins, many times influencing the outcome of games more than running backs or receivers. His speed and strength have lead him to post incredible sack numbers—something he's done more of than any other defensive player in the franchise's history.

He has put his personal stamp on the Pro Bowl, playing in all but one game since coming into the NFL in 1989. As the initial first round pick of the Schottenheimer era, Derrick led the Chiefs' resurgence to prominence, one of the major factors in the overall success of the team the last ten seasons.

1. Where did Thomas go to college?
2. What major award did he win following his senior season?
3. How many sacks did Thomas have his rookie season?
4. What is his all-time best sack total for a season?
5. What is his single-game best for sacks?
6. How many touchdowns has he scored in his career?
7. How many safeties has he scored?
8. How many consecutive Pro Bowls was Thomas selected for?
9. He's recovered 18 fumbles in his career. How many has Thomas forced?
10. How many interceptions does he have in his career?
11. Which quarterback has Thomas sacked the most in his career?
12. How many career sacks does Thomas have (through the 1998 season)?

Derrick Thomas

Johnny Robinson

Johnny Robinson

(1960-71)

Whenever you needed a big play, one that would break the other team's back, Johnny was there to make it.

Len Dawson

One of the first big playmakers on the Chiefs defense, Johnny Robinson was an integral part of the 1962, 1966 and 1969 championship teams. He is second on the team's all-time interception list, and led the league twice. He was named All-AFL five consecutive years.

"You have to have the mindset of a quarterback. Johnny had that. He was intuitive. He just had a knack for the game," Willie Lanier said of his teammate.

Johnny received one of his greatest honors when he was named to the AFL's All-Time team.

1. What college did Robinson attend?

2. What position did he first play for the Texans?

3. Robinson was a first-round pick of the Texans in 1960. What NFL team also picked him in the first round?

4. How many touchdowns did Robinson score for the Dallas Texans?

5. How many interceptions did Robinson have in his career?

6. How many interceptions did Robinson have in the 1962 AFL Championship game?

7. Robinson led the AFL in picks in 1966 and the NFL in 1970. How many interceptions did he have in those two seasons?

8. How many interceptions did Robinson have in Super Bowl IV?

9. Did Robinson play for any other teams after the Chiefs?

Buck Buchanan

(1963-75)

It was unbelievable how he could run for a big guy. Some big people are quick but are not fast. Other big people are are fast but not quick. He was both fast and quick...He was highly motivated to be the best.

Hank Stram
at Buchanan's Hall of Fame induction

He wasn't just big, he was fast and strong, a combination that led to the Hall of Fame. Like no one before him, the Grambling All-American changed the standard of how a defensive lineman is supposed to play, and also the kind of physical attributes needed to perform at an All-Pro level.

Buck Buchanan's presence on the field was always evident, and because of his tremendous size and strength, opponents would double-team or even triple-team him. It wouldn't matter—Buck would still make the play. He was one of the rock-solid leaders on the Chiefs throughout his career, and played a monster game in Super Bowl IV.

His importance to the Chiefs? He was twice voted the club's MVP by his teammates. Buck passed away on July 16, 1992.

1. Where did Buchanan go to high school?

2. What position did Buchanan play briefly before settling in at defensive tackle?

3. How many seasons in a row was Buchanan selected for the All-Star game?

4. How many seasons did Buchanan play for the Chiefs?

5. He was twice voted the team's MVP. What years did he win the award?

6. One of Buchanan's Grambling teammates played with the Chiefs in 1967-68. Who was this teammate?

7. How many sacks did Buchanan have in Super Bowl IV?

8. Did Buchanan play with any other teams during his career?

Buck Buchanan smashes Green Bay quarterback Bart Starr in Super Bowl I.

Abner Haynes

Abner Haynes

(1960-65)

He was a franchise player before they talked about franchise players.

Hank Stram
on Abner Haynes

A Dallas native, Abner Haynes helped put the new American Football League on the map and made a name for himself as well. Haynes wasn't just the franchise's first big star, he was also the AFL's first true superstar.

"He did it all—rushing, receiving, kickoff returns, punt returns," Hank Stram said of Haynes' talents. "He gave us the dimension we needed to be a good team in Dallas."

Abner spent five seasons with the Texans and Chiefs, and held numerous club records when he retired. In the team's three seasons in Dallas, he scored 43 touchdowns and totaled 4,472 rushing and receiving yards. He was the league's first Player of the Year in 1960.

1. Where did Haynes go to high school?

2. Where did Haynes go to college?

3. How many times did Haynes lead the league in rushing?

4. How many times did Haynes lead the league in touchdowns scored?

5. How many times did Haynes rush for more than 1,000 yards?

6. Haynes owns the franchise record for most touchdowns in a game with five. When and against what team did he score the five touchdowns?

7. Haynes was originally a first round pick by another AFL club. What team picked him?

8. What NFL team drafted Haynes?

9. How many times did Haynes lead the Texans/Chiefs in rushing?

10. What teams did Haynes play for after he left the Chiefs?

Mike Garrett

(1966-70)

His power is amazing, but his best attribute may be his great sense of balance with that tricky lateral movement. He's always under control.

Hank Stram
on Mike Garrett

The best of Hank Stram's scatbacks, Mike Garrett was a standout for the Chiefs from 1966 through the beginning of the 1970 season. He possessed lightning-quick moves, the ability to easily change directions without losing speed and was especially great at improvising in the middle of a run. He was always difficult to bring down.

When he chose the AFL over the NFL, he brought true star power to Kansas City and the league—his running in Super Bowl I befuddled the Packers, and his steady play in Super Bowl IV helped down the Vikings. Garrett ranks fifth on the Chiefs' list of career rushing leaders.

1. Where did Garrett play college football?

2. What prestigious college football award did he win following his senior season?

3. In what round of the AFL draft did the Chiefs pick Garrett?

4. What NFL team also drafted Garrett?

5. Did Garrett score in Super Bowl I?

6. What was Garrett's best single-game rushing performance?

7. How many times did Garrett lead the team in rushing yards for a season?

8. What was his highest single-season rushing total?

9. How many touchdowns did Garrett score for the Chiefs?

10. What team was Garrett traded to in 1970?

Mike Garrett

Ed Podolak

Ed Podolak

(1969-77)

He did not have what you call a natural athletic ability like the great, great running backs. Those guys run on skill alone, with no thought process. Ed had very good athletic abilities, but more important, he had an ability to understand the theory of the offense and how to make things work.

Jack Rudnay, 1989
on Ed Podolak

Okay, Ed Podolak played the game of his life on December 25, 1971. But it's unfair to remember his entire career with one game.

"If the game had never gone six quarters, no one would have known my name," said Podolak of his place in Chiefs' history. But it's not true. The Iowa Hawkeye's contributions to the Chiefs extended over the full balance of his playing time. Ed was the consummate do-everything back. He ran well, caught passes, returned kicks, even played on the special teams his first couple of years. His rushing stats aren't glittering numbers of incredible achievement, just steady, workman-like production that led to the main objective—winning football games. And that sustained, high-level of play throughout his career, not the 1971 playoff game, is Podolak's true legacy with the Chiefs.

1. Podolak played two positions at the University of Iowa. What were they?
2. In what round of the 1969 draft was Podolak selected?
3. How many times did Podolak rush for more than 100 yards in a game?
4. Podolak holds the Chiefs' record for punt returns in a game. How many did he have, when did he do it, and against what team did he set the record?
5. How many times did Podolak lead the league in average punt return yardage?
6. What's the most yards rushing Podolak had in a season?

7. How many times did Podolak lead the Chiefs in receptions?

8. Podolak piled up 350 total yards against the Dolphins in the 1971 Divisional Playoff game against the Dolphins. How many of those yards were rushing yards? Return yards? Passing receiving yards?

9. What's the most yards he gained rushing in a game?

10. How many passes did he throw for the Chiefs?

Otis Taylor

(1965-75)

His catches were splendid. I just can't describe them; I don't know enough adjectives. I don't know how even you people (sportswriters) can describe him.

Hank Stram, 1971
on Otis Taylor

Was there any pass thrown his way he didn't catch? The Prairie View A & M standout came to Kansas City and immediately provided a big-play punch. Otis made things happen.

He had speed, guile, quickness, tenacity and the penchant to make his biggest plays when the Chiefs needed them most. And he had hands. His clutch receptions in the 1969 AFL title game helped lead the Chiefs back to the Super Bowl, and his spectacular break-away effort for a touchdown in Super Bowl IV put the Vikings away. His entire 1971 season was big play after big play as Kansas City returned to the playoffs.

Diving catches, leaping and stretching receptions, passes caught with one hand. Otis Taylor is the Chiefs' greatest receiver of all-time.

1. Taylor had his jersey number retired at Prairie View A & M. What was his number?
2. In what round of the AFL draft did the Chiefs pick Taylor?
3. What NFL team wanted Taylor?
4. What special bonus did the Chiefs give Taylor for signing with them?
5. How many passes did Taylor catch in Super Bowl I?
6. How many did he catch in Super Bowl IV?
7. How many seasons did Taylor have more than 1,000 yards receiving?

Otis Taylor

8. How many touchdowns did Taylor score in his career?
9. How many times did Taylor lead the league in receiving yards?
10. How many Pro Bowls did Taylor play in?

Jan Stenerud

(1967-79)

Jan was awesome. We knew if we could get the ball to midfield, we could score.

Mike Garrett
on Jan Stenerud

A Norwegian ski jumper who came to the United States on a skiing scholarship, Jan Stenerud was at the forefront of the revolutionary changes the kicking game went through in pro football from the mid-1960s to the mid-1970s. Soccer-style kickers changed the range and accuracy factors for field goals, and Stenerud was the best of his time. Jan still owns or shares nine Chiefs records, including field goals attempted in a career and season. He finished his career with 17 field goals over 50 yards, played in six Pro Bowls, and was selected for the NFL's 75th Anniversary team. In 1991, Jan became the first "pure" placekicker inducted into the Pro Football Hall of Fame.

1. Where was Stenerud born?

2. Where did Stenerud attend college?

3. What was the distance of his longest field goal in college?

4. How many field goals did he have in his career? How many did he make for the Chiefs?

5. What two teams did he play for after leaving KC?

6. How many points did Stenerud finish with at the end of his career?

7. How many field goals did he make in Super Bowl IV?

8. What was the distance of the longest field goal in Super Bowl IV?

9. How long was the longest field goal of his professional career?

Jan Stenerud

Emmitt Thomas

Emmitt Thomas

(1966-78)

What you try to do is limit the opposition on crucial third down plays and stop the long touchdown pass. If you do that and we win the game, then you can say you've had a pretty good game.

Emmitt Thomas, 1972
on playing cornerback

He started as an undrafted free agent and ended as one of the Chiefs' all-time greats. A native of Angleton, Texas, Emmitt Thomas's improbable beginning gave way to a stellar career. When he retired, Thomas was the Chiefs' all-time team leader in interceptions with 58, set the team record for career interception return yardage with 938, and had been named to six Pro Bowl or AFL All-Star teams. Twice he led the league in picks, and during the 1969 playoffs, stole four passes that were vital in the Chiefs Super Bowl run, including one against the Vikings on Super Sunday. His consistent play at the right cornerback spot helped make the Chiefs' secondary one of the best ever during his tenure with the club.

1. Where did Thomas attend college?
2. How many touchdowns did Thomas score in his career?
3. How many times did he lead the league in interceptions?
4. What was his best single-season total?
5. During his rookie season in 1966, what special teams duty did Thomas perform?
6. How many games did he play in for the Chiefs?
7. How many interception return yards did Thomas compile in his career?
8. Thomas is currently (1999) the defensive coordinator for which NFL team?

Christian Okoye

(1987-92)

Nobody in this league has that kind of speed and power combination. There might be some guys faster, and there might be some guys out there who are nearly as strong. But none with that combination.

Irv Eatman, offensive lineman
on Christian Okoye

Was he real, or just a freight train in shoulder pads? He pounded and bruised and battered opposing teams for six seasons with Kansas City, earning one of the most formidable nicknames in the history of the NFL.

He was the Nigerian Nightmare.

Christian Okoye was the most overpowering running back to ever wear a Chiefs jersey. He didn't just carry the ball, he also carried would-be tacklers. His bullish running style, combined with his surprising speed, left defenders dazed and befuddled. He retired as the team's all-time leading rusher with 4,897 yards, and also holds the single-season record for most yards gained rushing at 1,480.

1. Where was Okoye born?

2. What college did he attend?

3. Okoye was selected in the second round of the 1987 draft. Who did the Chiefs select in the first round of that draft?

4. How many times in his career did he rush for more than 1,000 yards?

5. How many times did he lead the league in rushing?

6. How many touchdowns did he score in his career?

7. Okoye holds the club record for the most rushing attempts in a game. What is that record, and against what team did he set it?

8. How many passes did he catch in his career?

9. How many Pro Bowls did Okoye play in?

Christian Okoye

Deron Cherry

Deron Cherry

(1981-91)

Deron Cherry exemplifies all that is good in professional football.

Carl Peterson,Chiefs GM
on Deron Cherry

One of the great success stories in the history of the Chiefs, Deron Cherry made the most of the opportunities presented to him and became one of the finest free safeties ever to play football. He led the Chiefs in tackles four times and interceptions six times.

His pass coverage was always excellent, and he finished his career as the Chiefs third all-time interception leader. Cherry played in 148 games and was always a strong influence over the entire Chiefs' defense. He was inducted into the Chiefs Hall of Fame in 1995.

1. Where did Cherry go to college?
2. What degree did he receive?
3. What round of the draft did the Chiefs pick Cherry?
4. What was Cherry's primary position while trying to make the Chiefs the first time?
5. How many interceptions did Cherry have in his career?
6. What is his best single-season total of interceptions?
7. What is the most interceptions he's had in one game?
8. How many touchdowns did he have in his career?
9. How many Pro Bowls did he play in?
10. Cherry is a part-owner of what NFL franchise?

Art Still

(1978-87)

You might get 15 sacks, and as far as the run goes, you'll be weak ... You've got to be well-rounded, not just in sacks and pass rushing but against the run.

Art Still
on playing the defensive line

He was an unstoppable force when rushing the passer or stopping the run. A Pro Bowl standout, Art Still had the misfortune of playing for some of the Chiefs' weaker teams. He was still able to compile impressive statistics in tackles, sacks and fumble recoveries.

Third on the Chiefs' all-time sack list, Still made 992 tackles during his 10 seasons with Kansas City. His totals might have been higher if not for two strike seasons, or had he played with better all-around teams. Still was inducted into the Chiefs Hall of Fame in 1997.

1. Where did Still go to college?

2. Still was the second overall player taken in the 1978 draft. Who was the first?

3. What is the most sacks Still had in a single season?

4. How many sacks did he have in his career?

5. What's the most sacks he had in a game?

6. How many times was Still selected for the Pro Bowl?

7. How many times did Still lead the Chiefs in sacks?

8. How many times did he lead the Chiefs in tackles?

9. What team did Still play for his final two seasons in the NFL?

Art Still

Fred Arbanas

Fred Arbanas

(1962-70)

He was a real player, a guy who came to play every down.

Len Dawson
on Fred Arbanas

Detroit native Fred Arbanas didn't redefine the tight end position—he merely exemplified it. For the nine seasons he played with the Texans and Chiefs, he was the best tight end in the league, an honor officially bestowed upon him when he was named to the All-Time AFL team by the Pro Football Hall of Fame.

Fred lost most of the sight in one eye following the 1964 season—he not only overcame the setback, but continued to excel. His solid blocking and sure hands played a major role on both of the Chiefs' Super Bowl teams. He caught 198 passes during his career and scored 34 touchdowns.

Arbanas was inducted into the Chiefs Hall of Fame in 1972.

1. What college did Arbanas attend?
2. In what round did the Texans draft Arbanas?
3. How many total receiving yards did Arbanas accumulate in his career?
4. What's the highest number of receptions Arbanas had in a single season?
5. What's the highest number of touchdowns he scored in a season?
6. What NFL team drafted Arbanas?
7. Did Arbanas play for any other pro teams?
8. How many times Arbanas chosen for the All-AFL team?

Chris Burford

(1960-67)

Every pass route Chris ran was a perfect pass route. You could throw the ball and know two things—Chris would be in perfect position and if it was anywhere near him, he'd catch it.

Len Dawson
on throwing to Chris Burford

An original member of the Chiefs franchise, Chris Burford joined the Dallas Texans in 1960 as a first round pick. The native Californian's impact with the team and fledgling league was immediate. He pulled in 46 passes that first season and 51 the next. Burford quickly gained a reputation among his teammates, as well as the rest of the league, for running perfect pass routes. He also had a great pair of hands, and he used them a lot during his time with the Chiefs.

Burford led the franchise in pass receptions four times and ranks third on the Chiefs' all-time list. A big part of the '62 and '66 AFL Championship teams, he also holds the team record for the most touchdown receptions in a season. A member of the College Football Hall of Fame, Burford is also enshrined in the Chiefs Hall of Fame.

1. What college did Burford attend?
2. How many career touchdowns did he score for the franchise?
3. How many total receptions did he catch for the Chiefs?
4. What is his highest total of receptions for a single season?
5. What is the most receptions he caught in a single game?
6. What is the highest number of total yards gained receiving Burford had in a single season?
7. How many total receiving yards did he have for his career?
8. Burford led the franchise in receptions four times. What years were those?

Chris Burford

Ed Budde

Ed Budde

(1963-76)

Ed Budde stands for what pro football is all about.

Ed Podolak, 1976

The Michigan native came to the Chiefs in the first round of the 1963 draft. Fourteen seasons later, he retired as one of the greatest offensive lineman in the franchise's history. Among his numerous awards, Budde was the first lineman in the AFL to be named Offensive Player of the Week, an honor he received for his blocking prowess in the Chiefs use of the "T" formation against the Raiders in 1968.

A perennial pro bowler, Ed was considered the finest offensive guard in the AFL and was named to the All-Time AFL team by the Pro Football Hall of Fame. He was inducted into the Chiefs Hall of Fame in 1983.

1. What university did Budde attend?
2. What honor did Budde receive after his senior season?
3. What NFL team drafted Budde?
4. The Chiefs had two first round picks in 1963. Budde was one of the picks, who was the other one?
5. How many games did he play in for the Chiefs?
6. How many Pro Bowls did he play in? What years?
7. Did Budde ever score a touchdown in his professional career?

Joe Montana

(1993-94)

Watching him work the two-minute drill was like looking over the shoulder of an artist as he completes a fine painting. He never gets rattled, never shows concern. There is about him an attitude that is unbelievably contagious.

Marcus Allen
on Joe Montana

Is he the greatest quarterback of all-time? Maybe, but in Kansas City, he was simply the best quarterback the team had since Len Dawson. Montana will most be remembered for helping return the Chiefs to the AFC title game, and given a couple breaks over the course of the 1993 season, Super Joe might have led the Chiefs to the Super Bowl.

His short tenure in KC was about something more than numbers—it was about attitude. For the first time since the 1969 team, the Chiefs had a winning record in the playoffs. Even though it was evident Montana was lacking some of his former talents, he deserves a special place in Chiefs history as one of the best ever to play quarterback for the team.

1. In what round of the draft was Montana selected?
2. How many times was Montana the Super Bowl MVP?
3. What were the particulars of the Chiefs trade with the 49ers to acquire Montana?
4. How many times in the regular season did Montana pass for at least 300 yards when he was with the Chiefs?
5. In his two seasons with the Chiefs, how many touchdown passes did Montana throw?
6. Was Montana selected for the Pro Bowl when he was with KC?
7. How many other times was he selected for the Pro Bowl?
8. Montana lost the 1993 AFC Championship game with the Chiefs. How many times did he lose the NFC Championship Game as the quarterback of the 49ers?
9. How many games did Montana miss in his two years with KC?
10. How many passing yards did Montana have for the Chiefs?

Joe Montana

Neil Smith

Neil Smith

(1988-96)

I'm trying to knock the other quarterback out of the game. I just want to get him on the ground or knock the ball loose. If he gets hurt, it's his own fault.

Neil Smith, 1994
on rushing the quarterback

A major force on the Chiefs' defensive line for nine seasons, Neil Smith presented opponents with the unenviable task of trying to contain him with conventional blocking tactics. They usually didn't work. Neil recorded big-time sack numbers and logged numerous Pro Bowl appearances for his work, as well as helping the Chiefs reach the playoffs six straight seasons.

The second overall pick in the 1988 draft, Smith was slow to develop during his first year, but blossomed into a true defensive superstar. His defection to Denver not withstanding, Smith rates as the one of the best ever to man the Chiefs' defensive front line.

1. Where did Smith go to high school?
2. Where did he go to college?
3. How many times did Smith lead the Chiefs in sacks?
4. What's the most sacks he had in a single season with Kansas City?
5. How many touchdowns did he score with Kansas City?
6. How many interceptions did he make for the Chiefs?
7. How many times was he selected for the Pro Bowl while with the Chiefs?
8. How many career sacks did he have for the Chiefs?
9. Smith was the second overall pick in the 1988 draft. Who was first?

Jerry Mays

(1961-70)

The worst loss the Chiefs have ever suffered was to Green Bay (in Super Bowl I). That was total humiliation. But it also started us on our drive to the championship (winning Super Bowl IV) and it helped us to gain maturity.

Jerry Mays, 1971

A Dallas native, nobody took it harder than Jerry Mays when the Texans moved to Kansas City. But the standout defensive lineman made the proper mental adjustments and played outstanding defense until his retirement following the 1970 season.

Mays started his career as a defensive tackle and switched to defensive end where he continued to excel. And he was always proud of playing on an AFL team.

"I loved the AFL," Mays said. "It was part of me...I was AFL from start to finish."

Mays was named to the All-Time AFL team, and was inducted into the Chiefs Hall of Fame in 1971. Jerry died on July 17, 1994.

1. What university did Mays attend?

2. What NFL team also drafted Mays?

3. Mays started out as a defensive tackle. What year did he switch to defensive end?

4. How many games did Mays play in for the Chiefs?

5. How many touchdowns did Mays score in his career?

6. How many times was Mays selected to play in the Pro Bowl/AFL All-Star game? What years?

7. How many interceptions did he have in his career?

Jerry Mays

Elvis Grbac

Elvis Grbac

(1997-98)

"I believe in Elvis Grbac. This football team believes in Elvis Grbac."
Marty Schottenheimer

Tabbed as the Chiefs' quarterback of the future when he came to Kansas City before the 1997 season, Elvis Grbac has fought the injury bug more than opposing teams. But the Chiefs still believe he can lead them back to the playoffs, and further. A full season at the Chiefs' helm might be all it takes to catapult Grbac to stardom.

A four-year starter at Michigan during his college career, Grbac was the backup quarterback for the San Francisco 49ers before coming to Kansas City. Grbac tossed 11 touchdown passes in the 1997 season for the Chiefs, and completed 57% of his passes for 1,943 yards. He was the Chiefs' offensive co-captain in 1998, sharing the honor with Dave Szott.

1. What is Grbac's hometown?

2. Grbac guided the University of Michigan to two bowl game wins. What two bowls were they?

3. Grbac was drafted by the San Francisco 49ers in the 1993 draft. In what round did the 49ers select him?

4. Who caught Grbac's first NFL touchdown pass?

5. Who caught Grbac's first touchdown pass as a Chief?

6. How many touchdown passes has Grbac thrown in his career (through the 1998 season)?

7. How many rushing touchdowns does he have for Kansas City?

8. Grbac completed a 65-yard pass against Pittsburgh in 1998, his longest as a Chief. Who caught the pass?

9. What's the most touchdown passes Grbac has thrown in a game for the Chiefs?

Tony Gonzalez

(1997-99)

Tony has a lot of ability and can be one of the top players at his position in the National Football League. Tony ... has a lot of qualities you're looking for."

Keith Rowen
Chiefs tight end coach

Ready to become one of the elite players in the NFL, Tony Gonzalez set the Chiefs' single-season receptions record for tight ends in 1998. He'll catch a lot more in the upcoming seasons. His combination of outstanding leaping ability and strong blocking skills are a sure ticket to the Pro Bowl. He had 621 receiving yards for in 1998, and 989 for his career.

Gonzalez won the Chiefs prestigious Mack Lee Hill Award in 1997, presented each year to the team's top rookie.

1. Where did Gonzalez attend high school?

2. An All-American tight end at Cal-Berkley, what other sport did Gonzalez play for the Golden Bears?

3. The Chiefs traded up in the draft to obtain the 13th pick so they could get Gonzalez. What team did they trade with for the pick, and what were the details of the trade?

4. What's the most catches Gonzalez has had in one game?

5. How many passes did Gonzalez catch his rookie season?

6. Gonzalez broke the franchise record for the most receptions by a tight end with 59. Whose record did he break?

7. How many touchdowns has Gonzalez scored for the Chiefs?

8. How many passes did Gonzalez catch in the 1997 Playoff Game against the Broncos?

Tony Gonzalez

Chiefs Numbers

Individual Records

(through the 1998 season)

Rushing

Most Attempts, Career

1,246 Christian Okoye
1,158 Ed Podolak
932 Marcus Allen
792 Abner Haynes
762 Curtis McClinton

Most Attempts, Season

370 Christian Okoye, 1989
245 Christian Okoye, 1990
236 Mike Garrett, 1967
234 Joe Delaney, 1981
225 Christian Okoye, 1991

Most Attempts, Game

38 Christian Okoye vs. Green Bay, Dec. 10, 1989
37 Christian Okoye vs. Seattle, Nov. 5, 1989
35 Barry Word vs. L.A. Raiders, Dec. 22, 1991
33 Christian Okoye vs. Dallas, Oct. 22, 1989
33 Marcus Allen vs. L.A. Raiders, Dec. 24, 1994

Most Yards Gained, Career

4,897 Christian Okoye
4,451 Ed Podolak
3,837 Abner Haynes
3,698 Marcus Allen
3,246 Mike Garrett

Most Yards Gained, Season

1,480 Christian Okoye, 1989
1,121 Joe Delaney, 1981
1,087 Mike Garrett, 1967
1,053 Tony Reed, 1978
1,049 Abner Haynes, 1962

Most Yards Gained, Game

200 Barry Word vs. Detroit, Oct. 14, 1990
193 Joe Delaney vs. Houston, Nov. 15, 1981
192 Mike Garrett vs. N.Y. Jets, Nov. 5, 1967
170 Christian Okoye vs. Dallas, Oct. 22, 1989
169 Mike Garret vs. Denver, Dec. 17, 1967

Most Touchdowns Rushing, Career

44 Marcus Allen
40 Christian Okoye
39 Abner Haynes
34 Ed Podolak

Most Touchdowns Rushing, Season

13 Abner Haynes, 1962
12 Christian Okoye, 1989
12 Marcus Allen, 1993
11 Marcus Allen, 1997
10 Billy Jackson, 1981

Most Touchdowns Rushing, Game

4 Abner Haynes vs. Oakland, Nov. 26, 1961

Passing

Most Passes Attempted, Career

3,696 Len Dawson
2,430 Bill Kenney
1,751 Mike Livingston
1,616 Steve DeBerg
1,075 Steve Bono

Most Passes Attempted, Season

603 Bill Kenney, 1983
520 Steve Bono, 1995
493 Joe Montana, 1994
444 Steve DeBerg, 1990
438 Steve Bono, 1996

Most Passes Attempted, Game

55 Joe Montana vs. San Diego, Oct. 9, 1994
55 Steve Bono vs. Miami, Dec. 12, 1994
54 Joe Montana vs. Denver, Oct. 17, 1994
54 Steve Bono vs. San Diego, Sept. 29, 1996
52 Bill Kenney vs. Denver, Oct. 30, 1983

Most Passes Completed, Career

2,115 Len Dawson
1,330 Bill Kenney
934 Steve DeBerg
912 Mike Livingston
594 Steve Bono

Most Passes Completed, Season

346 Bill Kenney, 1983
299 Joe Montana, 1994
293 Steve Bono, 1995
258 Steve DeBerg, 1990\
256 Steve DeBerg, 1991

Most Passes Completed, Game

37 Joe Montana vs. San Diego, Oct. 9, 1994
34 Joe Montana vs. Denver, Oct. 17, 1994
33 Steve Bono vs. Miami, Dec. 12, 1994
31 Bill Kenney vs. San Diego, Dec. 11, 1983
30 Steve DeBerg vs. Cleveland, Nov. 24, 1991

Most Yards Gained, Career

28,507 Len Dawson
17,277 Bill Kenney
11,873 Steve DeBerg
11,295 Mike Livingston
6,489 Steve Bono

Most Yards Gained, Season

4,348 Bill Kenney, 1983
3,444 Steve DeBerg, 1990
3,283 Joe Montana, 1994
3,121 Steve Bono, 1995
3,115 Dave Krieg, 1992

Most Yards Gained, Game

435 Len Dawson vs. Denver, Nov. 1, 1964
411 Bill Kenney vs. San Diego, Dec. 11, 1983
397 Bill Kenney vs. New Orleans, Sept. 8, 1985
395 Steve DeBerg vs. Denver, Sept. 17, 1990
393 Joe Montana vs. Denver, Oct. 17, 1994

Most Touchdown Passes, Career

237 Len Dawson
105 Bill Kenney
67 Steve DeBerg

Most Touchdown Passes, Season

30 Len Dawson, 1964
29 Len Dawson, 1962
26 Len Dawson, 1963 & 1966
24 Len Dawson, 1967
24 Bill Kenney, 1983

Most Touchdown Passes, Game

6 Len Dawson vs. Denver, Nov. 1, 1964
5 Len Dawson vs. Boston, Sept. 25, 1966
5 Len Dawson vs. Miami, Oct. 8, 1967

Pass Receiving

Most Pass Receptions, Career

416 Henry Marshall
410 Otis Taylor
391 Chris Burford
377 Stephone Paige
352 Kimble Anders

Most Pass Receptions, Season

80 Carlos Carson, 1983
72 Andre Rison, 1997
68 Chris Burford, 1963
67 Kimble Anders, 1994
66 McArthur Lane, 1976

Most Pass Receptions, Game

12 Ed Podolak vs. Denver, Oct. 7, 1973
11 Chris Burford vs. Buffalo, Sept. 22, 1963
11 Emile Harry vs. Cleveland, Nov. 24, 1991
11 Kimble Anders vs. N.Y. Giants, Sept. 10, 1995

Most Yards Gained, Career

7,306 Otis Taylor
6,545 Henry Marshall
6,360 Carlos Carson
6,341 Stephone Paige
5,525 Chris Burford

Most Yards Gained, Season

1,351 Carlos Carson, 1983
1,297 Otis Taylor, 1966
1,110 Otis Taylor, 1971
1,092 Andre Rison, 1997
1,078 Carlos Carson, 1984

Most Yards Gained, Game

309 Stephone Paige vs. San Diego (8 rec.), Dec. 22, 1985
213 Curtis McClinton vs. Denver (5 rec.), Dec. 19, 1965
206 Stephone Paige vs. Denver (10 rec.), Sept. 17, 1990
197 Carlos Carson vs. San Diego (9 rec.), Oct. 25, 1987
190 Otis Taylor vs. Pittsburgh (6 rec.), Oct. 18, 1971

Scoring

Most Points, Career

1,466 Nick Lowery
1,231 Jan Stenerud
360 Otis Taylor
348 Abner Haynes
332 Chris Burford

Most Points, Season

139 Nick Lowery, 1990
129 Jan Stenerud, 1968
119 Jan Stenerud, 1969
116 Jan Stenerud, 1970
116 Nick Lowery, 1983

Most Points, Game

30	Abner Haynes vs. Oakland, Nov. 26, 1961
24	Frank Jackson vs. Denver, Dec. 10, 1961
24	Abner Haynes vs. Boston, Sept. 8, 1962
24	Frank Jackson vs. San Diego, Dec. 13, 1964
24	Bert Coan vs. Denver, Oct. 23, 1966

Team Records

Most Points Scored, Season

448	1966 season
408	1967 season
389	1962 season

Most Points Scored, Game

59	vs. Denver, Sept. 7, 1963
56	vs. Denver, Oct. 23, 1966

Most Touchdowns Scored, Season

55	1966 season
50	1962 season
49	1964 and 1967 seasons

Most Yards Gained Rushing, Season

2,986	1978 season
2,633	1981 season
2,407	1962 season

Most Yards Gained Passing, Season

4,341	1983 season
3,960	1994 season
3,568	1984 season

Fewest Points Allowed, Season

170	1968 season
177	1969 season
184	1982 season

Most Passes Intercepted By, Season

37	1968 season
33	1966 season
32	1960, 1962 and 1969 seasons

Chiefs vs. the NFL

Regular Season Opponents	**W**	**L**	**T**
Arizona Cardinals	4	1	1
Atlanta Falcons	4	0	0
Baltimore Ravens	0	0	0
Buffalo Bills	15	19	1
Carolina Panthers	1	0	0
Chicago Bears	3	4	0
Cincinnati Bengals	11	9	0
Cleveland Browns	7	8	2
Dallas Cowboys	3	4	0
Denver Broncos	44	35	0
Detroit Lions	5	3	0
Green Bay Packers	5	2	1
Indianapolis Colts	6	6	0
Jacksonville Jaguars	0	2	0
Miami Dolphins	10	13	0
Minnesota Vikings	4	3	0
New England Patriots	14	8	3
New Orleans Saints	4	3	0
New York Giants	2	7	0
New York Jets	15	14	1
Oakland Raiders	41	37	2
Philadelphia Eagles	2	1	0
Pittsburgh Steelers	7	15	0
St. Louis Rams	2	4	0
San Diego Chargers	40	37	1
San Francisco 49ers	3	4	0
Seattle Seahawks	27	14	0
Tampa Bay Bucs	5	2	0
Tennessee Oilers	26	17	0
Washington Redskins	4	1	0

Year-by-Year Results

Year	Record	Division Finish
1960	8-6	2nd AFL West
1961	6-8	2nd AFL West
1962	11-3	1st AFL West
1963	5-7-2	3rd AFL West
1964	7-7	2nd AFL West
1965	7-5-2	3rd AFL West
1966	11-2-1	1st AFL West
1967	9-5	2nd AFL West
1968	12-2	1st AFL West (tie)
1969	11-3	2nd AFL West
1970	7-5-2	2nd AFC West
1971	10-3-1	1st AFC West
1972	8-6	2nd AFC West
1973	7-5-2	2nd AFC West (tie)
1974	5-9	3rd AFC West (tie)
1975	5-9	3rd AFC West
1976	5-9	4th AFC West
1977	2-12	5th AFC West
1978	4-12	5th AFC West
1979	7-9	5th AFC West
1980	8-8	3rd AFC West (tie)
1981	9-7	3rd AFC West
1982	3-6	4th AFC West
1983	6-10	4th AFC West
1984	8-8	4th AFC West
1985	6-10	5th AFC West
1986	10-6	2nd AFC West
1987	4-11	5th AFC West
1988	4-11-1	5th AFC West
1989	8-7-1	2nd AFC West
1990	11-5	2nd AFC West
1991	10-6	2nd AFC West
1992	10-6	2nd AFC West
1993	11-5	1st AFC West
1994	9-7	2nd AFC West
1995	13-3	1st AFC West
1996	9-7	2nd AFC West
1997	13-3	1st AFC West
1998	7-9	4th AFC West

More Chiefs Trivia

Lamar Hunt

Lamar Hunt

(1960-Present)

No new league had succeeded since the turn of the century. Hunt was not, however, the sort of man to abandon a dream just because no one was selling what he wanted to buy.

Joe Foss, AFL Commissioner
on Lamar Hunt's determination

After several exasperating and disappointing attempts to acquire a franchise in the NFL, Lamar Hunt got the idea of a lifetime—starting a new pro football league. Hunt became the owner of the American Football League's Dallas Texans, and the leading architect in changing football history.

The new league was a way for Hunt to have a team in Dallas, but he did not foresee the NFL stepping in and adding the expansion Cowboys after his AFL club was ready to go. Lamar eventually came to the hard realization he would have to move the franchise, and Kansas City was the lucky choice for his team's new home.

While Hunt has added many things to the game of professional football, his most recognized contribution might be dubbing the AFL-NFL Championship Game the "Super Bowl."

1. Hunt attended SMU. What degree did he receive?

2. Hunt was a reserve on the SMU football team. What position did he play?

3. Hunt has been responsible for only one trade in the history of the franchise. What were the particulars of the deal?

4. When was Hunt inducted into Pro Football's Hall of Fame?

5. How many other sports franchises does he have a percentage in or own?

6. In addition to the Pro Football Hall of Fame, Hunt has been inducted into two other Halls of Fame. What sports do these halls represent?

7. Two states have also honored Hunt in their respective Sports Halls of Fame. What states have honored him?

Hank Stram

(1960-74)

He is the man. There is no in-between. But you talk to him and he puts the men on the field who should be there. I've never seen anyone who wants to win as much as he does.

Buck Buchanan
on Hank Stram

Coming from the unknown obscurity that only an assistant coach in the college ranks can have, Hank Stram took the reins of the newly formed Dallas Texans and catapulted himself to the top of the coaching world. He gave the world the "offense of the '70s," and more importantly, led the Chiefs to the 1969 World Championship.

Know as "Dapper," "the Mentor," and the "Little General," Stram always emphasized camouflage and variety in his coaching philosophy, but within a conservative frame. The "I" formation on offense and the triple stack on defense are just two of his many innovations, and both were major factors that resulted in the high point of his career, the Chiefs' Super Bowl win over the Vikings.

1. Where did Stram attend college?
2. How many colleges did he coach at before starting with the Texans?
3. How many years did Stram coach the Chiefs/Texans?
4. How many head coaching jobs did Stram have before taking the top spot with the Texans?
5. Stram always carried rolled up papers in his hand during games. What was on the papers?
6. Stram was a standout in two sports at his college. What were they?
7. What is the fewest amount of wins the Chiefs had under Stram, and in what year did they do it?
8. How many division championships did KC win under Stram?
9. What team did Stram coach after leaving the Chiefs?
10. What field did Stram enter after his coaching career?

Hank Stram

Gunther Cunningham

Gunther Cunningham

(1999-Present)

Gunther has earned this. I have every confidence that he's going to take this next step. He's prepared himself for this for a long time, and prepared himself well. And again, probably the most important aspect is I know how players respond to him.

Carl Peterson
on Gunther Cunningham

After toiling for years in the ranks of assistant coaches, Gunther Cunningham finally landed a head coaching position, and takes control of the Chiefs for the 1999 season. As the Chiefs' defensive coordinator from 1995-98, Cunningham put together one of the NFL's top defenses, leading the league in scoring defense in 1995 and 1997. The Chiefs won 13 games each of those years.

A hard worker with an intense desire to suceed, Cunningham is well-like and respected by his players.

"He knows how to command and create discipline," Carl Peterson said of his new head coach. "Overall, he's a leader, and that's obviously something you look for in a head coach." 1999 is Cunningham's 18th season as a coach in the NFL, and his 31st overall as a coach.

1. Where was Cunningham born?

2. Before attending the University of Oregon, what college did Cunningham attend?

3. What two positions did Cunningham play in college?

4. What was Cunningham's first coaching job?

5. How many different colleges did Cunningham work for?

6. Where was Cunningham's first professional coaching job? What did he do?

7. How many other NFL teams has Cunningham worked for?

8. How many times was he a defensive coordinator in the NFL?

Marty Schottenheimer

Marty Schottenheimer

(1989-98)

He is, without a doubt, the fiercest competitor I have ever known.

Carl Peterson
on Marty Schottenheimer

He couldn't add the Super Bowl to his list of accomplishments, but that's the only thing missing. In his ten seasons as the Chiefs' head man, Marty Schottenheimer achieved unparalleled success, but his failure to land in the big game always haunted him and his players.

He took over a Chiefs team with a long, sad history of losing — the year before he arrived the team posted only four wins. Ten years and seven playoff appearances later, Kansas City was again a formidable power in the NFL. The Chiefs experienced only one losing season during the Schottenheimer era, his last, and throughout his run as the Chiefs head coach, he maintained a consistent level of play from his teams. He retired with the highest winning percentage of any Chiefs coach, and when the whole of his career is examined, Schottenheimer's coaching prowess — minus the failure in the playoffs — stands second to only a few of his peers.

1. Where did Schottenheimer go to college?

2. An All-American coming out of college, Schottenheimer played in the College All-Star game and was drafted by both an NFL and AFL team. What two teams drafted him, and who did he sign with?

3, How many different teams did he play with in his career?

4. Before starting his coaching career, what did Schottenheimer do while living in Denver?

5. Schottenheimer's first coaching job was with what team?

6. For what three teams was Schottenheimer an assistant coach before becoming a head coach?

7. Schottenheimer became the head coach of the Browns midway through the 1984 season. How many games did his team win in his first full season as head coach?

8. How many times did the Browns win the AFC Central when he was head coach?

9. When did Schottenheimer take over the head coaching job at Kansas City?

10. How many division titles did he win at Kansas City?

11. How many games did he win as the Chiefs head coach?

12. What was his overall won-lost record?

13. What was his playoff record with the Browns?

14. What is his playoff record with the Chiefs?

15. What's the most games one of his teams won in one season?

16. Since 1960, only four other coaches have taken their teams to the playoffs as much or more than Schottenheimer. Who are the other four coaches?

The Playoffs

1. What opponents have the Chiefs played the most in post-season play?

2. What is the Chiefs' all-time record in the playoffs?

3. How many playoff games have the Chiefs had on their home field?

4. How many times have the Chiefs qualified for the playoffs?

5. How many AFC Western Division Championships have the Chiefs won?

6. How many AFL Championships did the Chiefs win?

7. Have the Chiefs ever won an NFL championship?

8. Through the 1998 season, four players have played in 10 post-season games for the Chiefs, the most in franchise history. Who are they?

9. Who has scored the most points in playoff history for the Chiefs?

10. Who has scored the most career post-season touchdowns?

11. Who holds the record for most yards gained rushing in a playoff game?

12. Who has thrown the most touchdown passes for the Chiefs in the post season?

13. What's the highest number of points the Chiefs have scored in a single playoff game?

14. What's the most points the Chiefs have allowed in a playoff game?

1968 Divisional Playoff
Kansas City, 6, at Oakland, 41
December 22, 1968

1. Why was there a Divisional Playoff in 1968?
2. How many touchdown passes did Daryle Lamonica throw for the Raiders?
3. Who was the Raiders top receiver in the game?
4. Who scored the Chiefs' points?
5. How many turnovers did the Chiefs have in the game?

1969 Divisional Playoff Game
Kansas City, 13, at New York Jets, 6
December 20, 1969

1. Why was there a Divisional Playoff in 1969?
2. What was the Jets' regular season record in 1969?
3. How many turnovers did the Chiefs have in the game?
4. How many turnovers did the Jets have in the game?
5. Who made the interceptions for the Chiefs?
6. Who scored the Chiefs' touchdown?
7. What were the distances of Stenerud's field goals?
8. How many yards passing did Joe Namath have? How many did Dawson have for Kansas City?

1971 AFC Divisional Playoff Game
Miami, 27, at Kansas City, 24
December 25, 1971

1. What was the official length of the game?
2. What was the Dolphins' record in 1971? What was the Chiefs record?
3. Who scored the first touchdown of the game for the Chiefs?
4. Who scored the Dolphins first touchdown?
5. How many field goals did Stenerud miss in the game?
6. How many turnovers did each team have?
7. Who was the Chiefs' leading rusher in the game?
8. Who was the Dolphins' leading rusher?
9. Who scored the Chiefs' second touchdown?
10. What was the distance of the game-winning field goal by Miami's Garo Yepremian?

1986 AFC Wild Card Playoff Game
Kansas City, 15, at New York Jets, 35
December 28, 1986

1. Why was the game played in New York?
2. Who was the Chiefs' starting quarterback in the game? Why?
3. Who scored the first touchdown of the game?
4. How many field goals did Nick Lowery attempt in the game?
5. How did the Chiefs score their second touchdown?

1990 AFC First Round Playoff Game
Kansas City, 16, at Miami, 17
January 5, 1991

1. What was Miami's regular season record in 1990?
2. Who scored the Chiefs' touchdown?
3. How many field goals did Lowery make?
4. Who scored the Miami's last touchdown?
5. Who was the Chiefs' leading rusher in the game?
6. How long was the field goal attempt Lowery missed at the end that would have won the game for the Chiefs?

Christain Okoye rips through the Dolphins in the 1990 playoffs.

1991 AFC First Round Playoff Game
Raiders, 6, at Kansas City, 10
December 28, 1991

1. What was the Chiefs' regular season record? What was the Raiders' record?
2. Who was the Raiders' starting quarterback in the playoff game?
3. How many interceptions did the Raiders' quarterback throw?
4. Who scored the Chiefs' touchdown, and how?
5. How many field goals did Lowery attempt in the game?
6. How many times did the Chiefs sack the Raiders' quarterback?

Nick Lowrey walks dejectedly from the field after missing on his game-winning field goal attempt at the end of the 1990 First Round Playoff game against Miami. The kick fell short, and the Chiefs lost, 17-16.

Chiefs quarterback Steve DeBerg hands to Barry Word during the 1991 First Round Playoff Game against the Raiders.

1991 AFC Divisional Playoff Game
Kansas City, 14, at Buffalo, 37
January 5, 1992

1. The Chiefs used two quarterbacks in the game. Who were they?
2. How many touchdown passes did Jim Kelly throw?
3. Who scored the Chiefs' touchdowns?
4. Who did the Bills defeat in the AFC Championship to advance to the Super Bowl?

1992 AFC First Round Playoff Game
Kansas City, 0, at San Diego, 17
January 2, 1993

1. Did the Chiefs beat the Chargers in the regular season?
2. Who won the AFC West in 1992?
3. Who scored the first touchdown in the playoff game for the Chargers?
4. Who was the Chiefs' starting quarterback in the game?
5. How many times did the Chargers sack KC's QB?

1993 AFC First Round Playoff Game
Pittsburgh, 24, at Kansas City, 27 (overtime)
January 8, 1994

1. Who scored the Kansas City's first touchdown?
2. Who was the Chiefs' leading rusher in the game?
3. How many turnovers did each team have?
4. The game went into overtime. How much time was left when the Chiefs tied the score?
5. Who scored the game-tying touchdown for the Chiefs?

Kevin Ross wraps up a Steelers' runner as Jay Taylor looks on in '93 playoff action.

6. How long was the game-winning field goal by Lowery?
7. How long was the overtime period?

Neil Smith sacks the Steelers' Neil O'Donnell and forces a fumble, but the Steelers recovered in the '93 playoff game.

Joe Montana takes a hit in the 1993 Divisional Playoff game at Houston, resulting in an interception. Tim Grunhard tries, to no avail, to lend a helping hand on the play.

1993 AFC Divisional Playoff Game
Kansas City, 28, at Houston, 20
January 16, 1994

1. The Chiefs lost to the Oilers early in the 1993 season. What was the score of that game?

2. The Oilers led, 10-0, at the half. Who scored the Chiefs' first touchdown in the third period to cut the lead?

3. Who was the Chiefs' leading rusher in the game?

4. How many touchdown passes did Montana throw in the game?

5. How many sacks did the Chiefs' defense have for the game?

6. Who scored the Chiefs' final touchdown?

1994 AFC First Round Playoff Game
Kansas City, 17, at Miami, 27
December 31, 1994

1. Who did the Chiefs defeat in their final two games to make the playoffs in 1994?
2. What was Miami's regular season record?
3. What was the score of the game at the half?
4. Who scored KC's first touchdown?
5. How many yards rushing did Marcus Allen have in the game?
6. How many turnovers did the Chiefs have in the game?

1995 AFC Divisional Playoff Game
Indianapolis, 10, at Kansas City, 7
January 7, 1996

1. Who did the Colts defeat for the right to play the Chiefs?
2. Who was the Colts starting quarterback?
3. Who scored the Chiefs' touchdown?
4. How many turnovers did the Colts have in the game?
5. Lin Elliott missed three field goals in the game. How many field goals did Colts kicker, Blanchard, miss?
6. How long was the last field goal Elliott missed?
7. How many turnovers did the Chiefs have in the game?

Marcus Allen runs against the Colts in the '95 playoff.

The Chiefs defense stopped the Colts throughout the 1995 Playoff game, but not when it counted most. Joe Phillips and Darren Mickell help out on the Colts runner.

1997 AFC Divisional Playoff Game
Denver, 14, at Kansas City, 10
January 4, 1998

1. What was the Broncos' regular season record in 1997?

2. How many turnovers did Denver have in the game?

3. Who scored the Chiefs' touchdown?

4. How many yards passing did Grbac have for the game?

5. Who was the Chiefs' leading rusher in the game?

6. How many yards rushing did Denver's Terrell Davis have?

After a good season, Steve Bono played poorly against the Colts in the 1995 Playoff game.

Jerome Woods sacks John Elway and forces a fumble in the 1997 playoff game against Denver.

7. How many times was Grbac sacked?

8. How much time was left when the Broncos scored their last touchdown?

AFL & AFC Championship Games

1962 AFL Championship Game
Dallas Texans, 20, at Houston Oilers, 17
December 23, 1962

Tommy Brooker's field goal in the second overtime period clinched the Dallas franchise's first AFL Championship. Because of the dramatic finish of the game, the fledgling league's image received a much needed boost. The Texans controlled the first half, the Oilers controlled the third and fourth quarters, and tied the game at 17-17 by the end of regulation. The first overtime game in the league's short history followed.

Despite kicking off into the wind to start the sudden-death overtime, the Texans held off the Oilers and won early in the sixth period on Brooker's kick, 20-17. Abner Haynes and Jack Spikes starred for Dallas.

1. Who was Houston's starting quarterback in the game?

2. What was the score at halftime?

3. Who was the Texans' leading rusher in the game?

4. Who was the Oilers' leading rusher in the game?

5. How many yards passing did Len Dawson have for Dallas?

6. Tommy Brooker kicked a field goal in the first quarter to open the scoring for the Texans. How long was it?

7. Who scored the Texans' touchdowns, and how?

8. How many yards passing did the Texans have in the game?

9. How many interceptions did the Texans have?

Tommy Brooker, Jim Tyrer, coach Hank Stram, Len Dawson and Abner Haynes celebrate their 1962 AFL Championship with team owner Lamar Hunt.

10. Who had the interception that set up the winning field goal?

11. What was the exact length of the game?

12. How long was the game-winning field goal by Brooker?

1966 AFL Championship Game
Kansas City, 31, at Buffalo, 7
January 1, 1967

The 1966 Chiefs brought Kansas City its first-ever major championship and snagged a spot in the first-ever Super Bowl by downing the Bills, 31-7. The game was played in frigid conditions, and after Buffalo fumbled away the opening kickoff, KC scored its first touchdown. The Bills tied the score, but were stopped the rest of the day as the Chiefs' defense shut down their attack.

1. What was the name of Buffalo's stadium where the game was played?

2. Who was Buffalo's starting quarterback?

3. Who scored the Chiefs' first touchdown?

4. Buffalo tied the game late in the first quarter on a long pass play. Who scored the touchdown for the Bills?

5. Who scored the Chiefs' second touchdown?

Dawson leads Garrett on a sweep against the Bills.

Otis Taylor hauls in a pass against Buffalo during the 1966 AFL Championship Game.

6. A 72-yard interception return setup a Chiefs field goal late in the second quarter and thwarted a possible Bills scoring opportunity. Who picked off the pass that led to the field goal?

7. What was the score at halftime?

8. How many yards passing did Len Dawson have in the game?

9. Who was the Chiefs' leading receiver in the game?

10. Who was the leading rusher for KC?

11. Who scored the Chiefs' last two touchdowns, and how?

12. How many sacks did the Bills record in the game?

1969 AFL Championship Game
Kansas City, 17, at Oakland, 7
January 4, 1970

After dropping two close, fiercely competitive games to the Raiders during the regular season, the Chiefs weren't given much of a chance to topple Oakland in the final AFL Championship Game. But spurred by a tremendous defensive effort and big plays from Len Dawson and Otis Taylor, the Chiefs surprised the Raiders and won the AFL title, 17-7.

The game was marred by some sloppy play in the fourth quarter as the two teams exchanged turnovers, but Kansas City hung onto the ball when they needed to and put the game away on a Stenerud field goal. The championship was the third for the Chiefs franchise, the most of any AFL team.

1. What was Oakland's regular season record in 1969?

2. The Raiders took the lead in the first quarter, 7-0. Who scored their touchdown?

3. Who was Oakland's starting quarterback?

Robert Holmes runs at the Raiders in the 1969 AFL title game.

4. Who scored the Chiefs' first touchdown, and how ?

5. How many yards passing did Dawson have for the game?

6. Who was the Chiefs' leading rusher in the game?

7. Who was the Raiders' leading rusher in the game?

8. What was the score of the game at the half?

9. Who scored the Chiefs' second touchdown?

10. How many field goals did the Raiders attempt in the game?

11. Who finished the game at quarterback for the Raiders?

12. How many times did the Chiefs lose fumbles in the game?

13. How long was the field goal Stenerud hit in the fourth quarter?

14. How many times did the Chiefs sack the Raider quarterbacks?

1993 AFC Championship Game
Kansas City, 13, at Buffalo, 30
January 23, 1994

Hoping there were magic moments yet to come from Joe Montana, the Chiefs took the field at Rich Stadium in Buffalo and fully expected to advance to the Super Bowl for the first time in 24 years. Reality settled over the team quickly though, as the Chiefs played poorly and lost to the Bills, 30-13. Buffalo ran up and down the field on KC, amassing 229 yards rushing. Montana suffered a concussion early in the third quarter and never returned to the game, effectively ending any chance KC had at making a comeback.

It was a disappointing end to a spectacular season. The Chiefs returned, finally, to the heights of their glory days in the 1960s. Montana and Marcus Allen had added much to the offense, and the defense, despite its poor performance in the AFC Championship Game, was considered one of the best in the league.

1. Who did the Chiefs defeat to advance to the 1993 AFC Championship game?

2. Who scored the game's first touchdown?

3. Nick Lowery kicked two field goals in the first half. What were the distances of the kicks?

4. How many yards passing did Joe Montana have in the game?

5. Who replaced Montana at quarterback, and how many yards passing did he have?

6. Who was the Chiefs' leading rusher?

7. Who scored the Chiefs' touchdown?

8. How many touchdowns did Buffalo's Thurman Thomas score?

9. How many times were the Chiefs' quarterbacks sacked?

10. Who was the Chiefs' leading receiver?

The Super Bowls

The Chiefs represented the AFL in the first ever Super Bowl and lost rather convincingly to the mighty Green Bay Packers. After regrouping, reviewing and retooling, Kansas City returned three years later for Super Bowl IV and faced the Minnesota Vikings. The team had learned their lessons well from the defeat to the Packers, and handily vanquished the Vikings, as well as embarrassing the entire NFL. The Chiefs won a well-deserved World Championship.

Kansas City hasn't made it back to the big game since that wondrous January afternoon in 1970, but they've been highly competitive the last decade. It's only a matter of time before the football gods again smile on the Chiefs and return them to the ultimate game.

Super Bowl I
Kansas City, 10, Green Bay, 35 at Los Angeles
January 15, 1967

Nobody around here is getting shook up because Green Bay is a 13-point favorite. Where do they get that? Just because we come from the American Football League?

Curtis McClinton, Chiefs Fullback
before Super Bowl I

It wasn't called the Super Bowl, officially anyway, and while most of America's football fans were excited about the game, they didn't really understand that this first inter-league matchup was the birth of what would soon become the premier sporting event in the USA.

Hank Stram & Vince Lombardi before Super Bowl I.

The Chiefs had the privilege (or was it a punishment?) of representing the AFL in Super Bowl I (officially called the AFL-NFL World Championship Game, for you purists). The funny thing is

Otis Taylor beats the Packer secondary in Super Bowl I action.

that while nobody expected Kansas City to win, nobody expected *anyone* to beat the Packers. They were, well, the Packers—considered then to be the greatest football team of all time.

The 1966 Chiefs were left with a place in history that has sometimes judged them harshly and other times fairly, but always as the losers of the first Super Bowl.

1. What was the official attendance of the Super Bowl I?
2. Who did the Packers defeat in the NFL Championship Game to get to the Super Bowl?
3. What was the Packers' regular season record in 1966?
4. What was the NFL's nickname for the AFL?
5. Who was the Packers' starting fullback in Super Bowl I?
6. Who was the Chiefs' starting fullback in Super Bowl I?
7. Who was the Chiefs' leading rusher in the game?
8. Who was the Packers' leading rusher?
9. Who scored the first touchdown in Super Bowl history?
10. Who scored the Chiefs' touchdown?

Dawson eludes Green Bay's Ray Nitschke in Super Bowl I.

Chris Burford runs from Packer Dave Robinson after catching a pass in Super Bowl I.

11. What was the score of the game at halftime?

12. How many times did the Packers sack the Chiefs' quarterback?

13. Who recorded the first sack in Super Bowl history?

14. How many times did the Chiefs sack the Packers' quarterback?

15. Who was the Chiefs leading receiver in the game?

16. How many yards rushing did Mike Garrett have?

17. The Chiefs picked off one of Starr's passes in the game. Who made the interception for KC?

18. Who was the Packers' leading receiver?

19. A Kansas City defensive back was knocked out of the game. Who was he?

20. How many yards passing did Dawson have?

21. Who was the MVP of Super Bowl I?

Super Bowl IV
Minnesota, 7, Kansas City, 23 at New Orleans
January 11, 1970

The good thing about this game is that we don't have to answer for it for the next three years as we did the last time.

Len Dawson, Chiefs Quarterback
after Super Bowl IV

Super Bowl IV was the sweetest of retributions for the Chiefs. They were again major underdogs in a big game, and the AFL was still considered inferior and uncompetitive by the NFL establishment. But this time the Chiefs were hardened with the battle scars of unmet expectations, and they did not forget the misery of losing to the Packers. Kansas City went to New Orleans *knowing* they would win the game, an attitude gained from three years of waiting to return to the championship game. And this time they dominated.

If the Chiefs' legacy of the first Super Bowl was to be remembered as losers, then the Chiefs of Super Bowl IV will always be remembered for showing the football world, once and for all, that the AFL *was* the equal of the NFL. The 1969 Kansas City Chiefs danced off the field at

Mike Garrett breaks into the end zone in Super Bowl IV.

Frank Pitts rips the Vikings on a reverse run during Super Bowl IV.

Buck Buchanan and Curly Culp sack Vikings quarterback Joe Kapp.

Tulane Stadium as the victors, owners of the Super Bowl Trophy (not yet called the Lombardi Trophy) and writers of the final chapter of the AFL's history, written with the blood of the Minnesota Vikings.

1. The Chiefs were big underdogs going into Super Bowl IV. How much were they supposed to lose by?

2. What was the official attendance of Super Bowl IV?

3. Who did the Vikings defeat in the NFL Championship game to get to Super Bowl IV?

4. What was the Vikings regular season record?

5. Who was Minnesota's starting quarterback?

6. Who was KC's leading rusher in the game?

7. Who was Minnesota's leading rusher?

8. How many times did the Chiefs sack the Minnesota quarterback?

9. How many times were the Chiefs' quarterbacks sacked?

10. How many passes did the Chiefs intercept, and who made them?

11. Jan Stenerud kicked three field goal in the game. What were the distances of the field goals?

12. Who scored the Chiefs' first touchdown?

13. What was the name of the play used to score the first touchdown?

14. Who was KC's leading receiver in the game?

15. Who was Minnesota's leading receiver?

16. Who scored the Vikings' touchdown?

17. Who scored the Chiefs' second touchdown? How?

Len Dawson hands off to Wendall Hayes in Super Bowl IV.

Jan Stenerud boots the first of his three field goals in Super Bowl IV.

18. What was the score at halftime?

19. Mike Livingston replaced Len Dawson late in the game. Who was Minnesota's backup quarterback?

20. How many times did the Chiefs punt in the game?

21. Who was the MVP of Super Bowl IV?

Stadiums

The Chiefs have used three different stadiums as their home field since coming into existence in 1960. Municipal Stadium served the team well after the move from Dallas, and the Chiefs enjoyed several big wins on that field. In the beginning, Arrowhead Stadium was strangely indifferent to the Chiefs, and it was more than a decade before they started to win there on a regular basis. It has become, in the last decade, one of the most formidable home fields in the NFL, and provides the Chiefs with a terrific advantage against their opponents.

Municipal Stadium

1. How many years did the Chiefs play at Municipal Stadium?

2. What was the stadium's original name?

3. What other names did the stadium go by before it was called Municipal Stadium?

Municipal Stadium circa 1966, the Chiefs' first home in Kansas City.

A sellout crowd for the Chiefs at Municipal Stadium.

4. What football team played in Municipal Stadium before the Chiefs, and when?

5. When was the first professional football game played in Municipal?

6. Who did the Chiefs play in their first game at Municipal?

7. What was the score? The attendance?

8. What was the original capacity of Municipal Stadium for baseball games?

9. What was the capacity the last year the Chiefs played in Municipal?

10. Who did the Chiefs beat for their final victory at Municipal?

11. What was the team's all-time record at Municipal Stadium in the regular season?

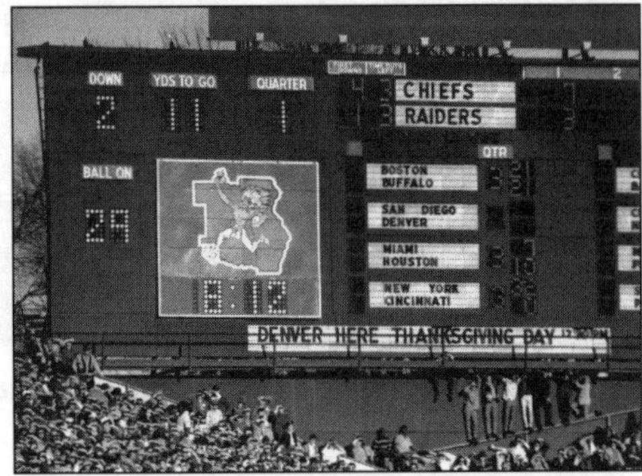

The main scoreboard at Municipal Stadium during the 1969 season.

Arrowhead Stadium

1. When was Arrowhead offi-

cially dedicated?

2. How many games did the Chiefs lose in Arrowhead before finally winning?

3. Who scored the first touchdown in Arrowhead?

4. Who kicked the first field goal?

5. How many times have the Chiefs gone undefeated during the regular season at Arrowhead?

6. What other professional team plays home games at Arrowhead?

7. What is the largest crowd ever at Arrowhead, and when?

8. What year was grass installed at Arrowhead Stadium?

9. How many playoff games have the Chiefs won in Arrowhead?

Arrowhead Stadium

End zone view of Arrowhead during the 1998 season.

Other Stadiums

1. What stadium did the Texans use as their home field in Dallas?

2. The Texans played pre-season games in three other Texas cities. What cities did they play in?

3. Kansas City played two pre-season games in Wichita, Kansas. What is the name of the stadium they played in?

4. What is the name of the stadium in Birmingham, Alabama, where the Chiefs played an exhibition game?

5. The Chiefs and Bears played an exhibition game on what college campus in 1972?

The Chiefs' first mascot, Warpaint, on a ride at Arrowhead.

Chiefs mascot, KC Wolf, entertains the fans during a game at Arrowhead.

Uniforms

From the first season in Dallas when Hank Stram helped pick the colors and uniform design of the Texans through the Schottenheimer teams of the 1990s, very little has changed in regards to the Chiefs uniforms. There have been minor variances, simple changes and updates made through the years, but the Chiefs uniforms have always been, more or less, the same: classic and timeless.

1. What color were the Dallas Texans' uniforms?
2. What was the logo on the Texans' helmet?
3. What was the one significant change made to the uniforms when the Texans became the Chiefs?
4. When did player names first appear on the back of the Chiefs/Texans jerseys?
5. One change was made to the Chiefs' jerseys from 1967 to 1968. What was it?
6. What year did the Chiefs first wear red pants on the road?
7. The Chiefs wore a special patch on the their jersey sleeve in Super Bowl IV. What was on the patch?
8. What was the last season the Chiefs wore red pants on the road?
9. The Chiefs made a minor change to their 1972 home uniforms. What was it?
10. The Chiefs wore a special patch on their jerseys during the 1994 season. What was the significance of the patch?

Chiefs home uniforms in the 1960s.

Chiefs road uniforms in the 1970s and 1980s.

Chiefs home uniforms in the 1990s.

Chiefs road uniforms in the 1990s.

Uniform Numbers

1. There are two numbers that have been worn by only one player in the history of the franchise. What are the numbers, and who wore them?

2. Willie Lanier wore number 63, which is now retired in his honor. What other Chief defensive great wore number 63 after Willie, but before it was retired?

3. How many jersey numbers have been retired by the Chiefs? What are the numbers, and who wore them?

4. How many players have worn number 13? Who are they?

5. What two numbers did Joe Montana want to wear before settling on 19?

6. What other quarterback wore number 19 for the franchise?

7. Marcus Allen wore number 32. What running back in the 1960s wore number 32?

8. What number did Emmitt Thomas wear? Two other players wore his number, too. Who were they?

9. What number did Robert Holmes wear?

10. Warren Moon will be number 1 for the Chiefs. Name at least two other players who wore number 1.

11. What number did Stephone Paige wear?

12. What number did Barry Word wear?

Quarterbacks

1. Who was the Texans first starting quarterback?

2. The Chiefs drafted this USC quarterback in the first round of the 1964 AFL draft. Who is he?

3. Who was Len Dawson's primary backup on the 1962 Texans?

4. From 1984 through 1986, The Chiefs shifted back and forth between two different starters for various reasons. Who were the two quarterbacks?

5. Who was the Chiefs' starting quarterback in 1995-96?

6. Only two quarterbacks have thrown for more than 400 yards in a game? Who are they, and when did they do it?

7. What Chiefs' quarterback holds the career record for highest completion percentage (at least 1,000 attempts)?

8. What quarterback threw the longest touchdown pass for the Chiefs? When and to whom?

9. Two quarterbacks hold the team record for the most pass attempts in a game. Who are they?

10. How many times have the Chiefs drafted a quarterback in the first round of the draft?

11. Who was the Chiefs backup quarterback in 1967, 1968 and the beginning of 1969?

12. When did Mike Livingston start his first game at quarterback for the Chiefs?

13. What college did Livingston attend?

14. After sharing playing time with Len Dawson for a few seasons, Mike Livingston was the team's number one quarterback from 1976 through 1978. Who became the Chiefs' starting quarterback in 1979?

Bill Kenney

15. Kansas City had a different starting quarterback each year in 1991, 1992 and 1993. Who were they?

Colleges

1. Two starters on the Super Bowl IV Championship team played together at Prairie View A&M. Who are they?

2. Bert Coan and Curtis McClinton played together for the Chiefs in Super Bowl I, and also together at what school?

3. Two Heisman Trophy winners from USC have played for the Chiefs. Who are they?

4. What college did Bill Maas attend?

5. Ed Budde and his son, Brad, both played for the Chiefs. What schools did they go to?

6. What college did Henry Marshall attend?

7. Where did Steve DeBerg go to college?

8. Mike Adamle, Jack Rudnay and Fred Williamson all attended the same school. What is it?

9. Albert Lewis, Leonard Griffin, Fred Jones, Ernie Ladd and Goldie Sellers all attended this school. What is it?

10. Name the college for each of the following players:

    Dino Hackett
    Tim Grunhard
    Frank Pitts
    Carlos Carson
    Neil Smith
    Pete Beathard
    Barry Word
    Jonathan Hayes

Jack Rudnay

Nick Lowery
Gary Spani
Bill Kenney
Mike Bell
Jerrel Wilson
Gary Barbaro
Emile Harry

The Defense

1. Which Chiefs team allowed the fewest points in a season?

2. Which Chiefs team allowed the most points in a season?

3. What is the most sacks the Chiefs have recorded in a season?

4. As a team, what's the most interceptions the Chiefs have made in a season?

Willie Lanier (63), Jim Lynch (51) and Buck Buchanan (86) rack up a Houston runner in a 1969 game.

5. What is the club record for fewest yards allowed rushing in a game?

6. What is the club record for most yards allowed rushing in a game?

7. What is the fewest amount of passing yards given up by the Chiefs in a game?

8. What is the most passing yards given up by the Chiefs in a game?

9. Who is the Chiefs all-time interception leader?

Jim Lynch

10. Who is the all-time leader in fumbles recovered for the Chiefs?

Running Backs

1. Who is the Chiefs all-time leader in rushing yardage?

2. Who was the Chiefs top rusher in 1963, the team's first season in Kansas City?

3. Six players have run for more than 1,000 yards in a season for the Chiefs. Who are they, and when did they do it?

4. Who holds the Chiefs' record for most rushing touchdowns in a season?

5. The longest run from scrimmage by a Chiefs player is 84 yards. What running back holds this record?

6. Who holds the Chiefs career record for most touchdowns scored rushing?

7. This running back is the only Chief to lead the league in pass receptions. Who is he and when did he do it?

Curtis McClinton

8. Who holds the Chiefs' record for the most 100-yard games in a season?

9. How many times have the Chiefs had a running back lead the league in rushing yards?

10. The Chiefs record for most consecutive games rushing for a touchdown is five. Who holds the record and when did he set it?

Wide Receivers

1. Who is the Chiefs' all-time leader in receptions?

2. Who holds the Chiefs' record for the most receptions in a season?

3. Who has the most touchdown receptions in a career?

4. Who has the most touchdown receptions in a season?

Stephone Paige

J.T. Smith

5. The Chiefs' record for the most touchdown receptions in a game is four. Who holds the record and when did it happen?

6. Who holds the Chiefs' record for the most receiving yards in a season?

7. Who is the Chiefs' all-time leader in career receiving yards?

8. Who holds the Chiefs' record for the most receiving yards gained in a game?

9. Only four Chiefs receivers have gone over the 1,000 yard mark in receiving yards for a season. Who are they?

Coaches

1. Who replaced Hank Stram as Chiefs head coach?
2. Who served the shortest time as Chiefs head coach?
3. How many seasons was Marv Levy a Chiefs head coach?
4. What was Levy's record with the Chiefs?
5. Only three head coaches have taken the Chiefs to the playoffs. Who are they?
6. Who replaced Marv Levy as Chiefs head coach?
7. How many head coaches have the Chiefs had?
8. How many Chiefs head coaches have had a winning record?
9. How many different coaching jobs did Gunther Cunningham have before he was named top man for the the Chiefs?

John Mackovic

Hank Stram

Todd Blackledge

Mike Bell

Tony Gonzalez

Paul Palmer

The Draft

1. The Chiefs had two first round picks in 1963. Who were they?

2. Who was the team's first pick in the 1965 draft?

3. The Chiefs drafted three receivers in the 1965 draft and all three made significant contributions in their time with the Chiefs. Who were they?

4. Who was the Chiefs' top pick in the 1969 draft?

5. The Chiefs traded their top pick in the 1975 draft to Houston. Who did they receive for the pick?

6. Who was the Chiefs' first-round pick in 1987?

7. Who was the Chiefs' first-round pick in 1981?

8. The Chiefs had two first-round picks in 1984. Who were they?

9. Who was KC's number one pick in the 1994 draft?

10. In what round of the 1990 draft was Dave Szott picked?

11. Who were the Chiefs' first two picks in the 1990 draft?

Kickers

1. Who was the Texans' first field goal kicker?
2. Who was the team's field goal kicker the first year in KC?
3. The Chiefs traded for a kicker in the middle of the 1966 season. Who did they pick up?
4. Who was the team's first punter?
5. What kicker holds the team record for the most points scored in a season?
6. What's the team record for the most field goals in a season?
7. Who holds the single-season punt average record, and when did he do it?
8. Who has the highest career punt average?
9. Who kicked the longest punt in team history?
10. Who has kicked the most field goals in a game? Most attempts?
11. Who has the most punts in a game?
12. Who has the most punts in a season for the Chiefs?
13. Who holds the club record for the most punts in a career?

Nick Lowery

Louie Aguiar

Jerrel Wilson boots one against the Redskins in 1971.

What Position Did They Play?

Name of the position each of the following players played.

1. Gary Barbaro
2. James Saxon
3. Pete Beathard
4. Elmo Wright
5. Morris Stroud
6. Joe Valerio
7. Jerry Blanton
8. Marvin Upshaw
9. Lloyd Burress
10. Tom Condon
11. Curley Culp
12. Jack Spikes
13. J. T. Smith
14. Charlie Getty
15. Bobby Hunt
16. Gloster Richardson
17. Frank Jackson
18. Ken Kremer
19. Tony Reed
20. Willie Mitchell

Nicknames

1. Who was the Hammer?
2. Who was called Pyscho?
3. Who was The Truck?
4. Christian Okoye was called the Nigerian Nightmare. What was his other nickname?
5. Who was called Honey Bear by his teammates?
6. What is Buck Buchanan's real first name?
7. Who was the Super Gnat?
8. What is Dino Hackett's real full name?

E. J. Holub

9. E. J. Holub was known as the Holler Guy. What does the E. J. stand for?
10. Who was called The Tank?

The Answers

Chiefs Players Trivia

Len Dawson

1. Alliance, Ohio
2. Yes
3. Pittsburgh and Cleveland
4. First round by the Steelers
5. Four
6. 83.2
7. 239
8. 237
9. Four – 1962 with 29, 1963 with 26, 1965 with 21, 1966 with 26
10. 30 in 1964
11. Nine
12. 2,879 in 1964
13. 28,711
14. 1962, 1964-69, 1975
15. Six to AFL game, once to Pro Bowl
16. 1962
17. *Inside the NFL* on HBO

Marcus Allen

1. San Diego's Lincoln High
2. Darrin Nelson of Stanford and Gerald Riggs of Arizona State
3. 12 wins, 10 losses
4. Nine wins, one loss
5. 173 on 24 carries against the Broncos on Nov. 24, 1985
6. 191 on 20 carries in Super Bowl XVIII against the Redskins
7. 132 against the Raiders on Dec. 24, 1994
8. 94 yards against the Colts on Jan. 7, 1995
9. 123
10. 44, a franchise record
11. 145, second behind Jerry Rice going into the 1998 season
12. Two: one against the Steelers on Nov. 3, 1997 (14 yards), and one against the 49ers on Nov. 30, 1997 (1 yard)
13. Three
14. Once, 1994
15. Greg Hill with 550 yards
16. 222
17. 587
18. Walter Payton with 3,838. Marcus is second with 3,022.

Bobby Bell

1. Cleveland High in Shelby, North Carolina
2. Quarterback, he was an all-state performer
3. University of Minnesota
4. Outland Trophy
5. Seventh
6. Yes, the Vikings drafted him in the second round
7. Defensive end
8. Eight

Willie Lanier

1. Morgan State
2. Tangerine
3. The second round of the 1967 draft
4. Seven: two AFL games and five Pro Bowls
5. 27
6. Five in 1975
7. 15, tied for third in club history
8. Honey Bear and Contact
9. Two

Derrick Thomas

1. Alabama
2. Butkus Award for best linebacker
3. 10
4. 20 in 1990
5. Seven vs. Seattle on Nov. 11, 1990
6. Four
7. Three
8. Nine
9. 42
10. None
11. John Elway of Denver, 17 times
12. 119.5

Johnny Robinson

1. LSU
2. Halfback
3. Detroit Lions
4. 15
5. 57

6. Two returned for 50 yards
7. 10 in each season
8. One
9. No

Buck Buchanan

1. Parker High in Birmingham, Alabama
2. Defensive end
3. Eight
4. 13
5. 1965 and 1967
6. Ernie Ladd
7. One
8. No

Abner Haynes

1. Lincoln High in Dallas
2. North Texas State in Denton, Texas
3. Once, 1960 with 875 yards
4. Once, with 19 in 1962
5. Once, 1962 with 1,049 yards
6. Oakland on Nov. 26, 1961. Dallas won the game, 43-11
7. Oakland
8. The Steelers drafted him in the fifth round
9. Four, 1960-62 & 1964
10. Denver Broncos, Miami Dolphins and New York Jets

Mike Garrett

1. University of Southern California
2. The Heisman Trophy
3. 20th
4. LA Rams
5. No
6. 192 yards on 23 carries vs. the Jets on Nov. 5, 1967
7. Three times – 1966, 1967 and 1969
8. 1,087 yards in 1967
9. 32
10. San Diego Chargers

Ed Podolak

1. Halfback and Quarterback
2. Second
3. 11
4. Eight, Nov. 10, 1974 vs. San Diego
5. Once, in 1970 with a 13.5 yard average
6. 749 in 1970
7. Three times, 1973-75
8. 85 rushing, 155 on returns, 110 receiving
9. 146 yards on 23 carries against the Chargers in San Diego on Oct. 27, 1974
10. He completed four of six attempts in his career for 82 yards

Otis Taylor

1. 17
2. Fourth
3. The Philadelphia Eagles
4. A red T-bird
5. Four for 57 yards
6. Six for 81 yards
7. Twice, 1966 and 1971
8. 57
9. Once, in 1971 with 1,110 yards
10. Three

Jan Stenerud

1. Fetsund, Norway
2. Montana State
3. 59 yards
4. He finished with 373 field goals, 279 with the Chiefs
5. Green Bay Packers and Minnesota Vikings
6. 1,699
7. Three
8. 48 yards
9. 55 yards

Emmitt Thomas

1. Bishop College
2. Five
3. Twice
4. 12 in 1974
5. He returned kickoffs.
6. 181
7. 938 yards on 58 interceptions
8. The Green Bay Packers

Christian Okoye

1. Enugu, Nigeria
2. Azusa-Pacific
3. Paul Palmer of Temple
4. Twice, 1989 and 1991
5. Once, 1989
6. 40
7. 38 rushing attempts against Green Bay on Dec. 10, 1989

8. 42
9. Two, 1989 and 1991

Deron Cherry

1. Rutgers
2. Biology
3. None. He was signed as a free agent.
4. Punter
5. 50
6. Nine in 1986
7. Four vs. Seattle on Sept. 29, 1985 (tied an NFL record)
8. Three
9. Six
10. Jacksonville Jaguars

Art Still

1. University of Kentucky
2. Earl Campbell of Texas, chosen by the Oilers
3. 14.5 in 1980 and again in 1984
4. 72.5
5. Four, against Oakland on Oct. 5, 1980
6. Four times, 1980-82 and 1984
7. Six times during his career
8. Three times
9. Buffalo

Fred Arbanas

1. Michigan State
2. Seventh
3. 3,101 yards
4. 34, in 1963 and 1964
5. Eight in 1964
6. The St. Louis Cardinals in the second round
7. No
8. Five, 1962-65 and 1967

Chris Burford

1. Stanford
2. 55 TDs
3. 391 receptions
4. 68 receptions in 1963
5. 11 vs. Buffalo on Sept. 22, 1963
6. 850 yards in 1961
7. 5,505 yards receiving
8. 1961-63, 1965

Ed Budde

1. Michigan State
2. His chosen for the All-America team
3. Philadelphia Eagles in Round 1
4. Buck Buchanan
5. 177 games
6. Seven, 1964, 1967-72
7. no

Joe Montana

1. Third by the 49ers in 1979
2. Three times
3. The Chiefs traded their 1993 first round draft pick to the 49ers for Montana, safety David Whitmore and a third round pick in the '94 draft.
4. Four
5. 29: 13 in '93 and 16 in '94
6. Yes, 1994
7. Seven, he was selected eight times overall
8. Two: 1983 to Washington, 24-21; and 1990 to New York, 15-13.
9. Seven games
10. 5,427 yards

Neil Smith

1. McDonough High in New Orleans
2. Nebraska
3. Four times, 1992 (with D. Thomas), 1993-95
4. 15 in 1993
5. Two
6. Three
7. Five times, 1991-95
8. 86
9. Aundray Bruce, chosen by Atlanta

Jerry Mays

1. SMU
2. Minnesota Vikings in the 11th round
3. In the middle of the 1964 season
4. 140 games
5. one, on a fumble recovery in 1963
6. six, 1962, 1964-68
7. one, in 1961

Elvis Grbac

1. Cleveland, Ohio
2. 1993 Rose Bowl and 1991 Gator Bowl
3. Eighth
4. Marc Logan on a one-yard pass
5. Kimble Anders on a five-yard pass
6. 34
7. 1

8. Derrick Alexander
9. 3, against Carolina on Sept. 21, 1997

Tony Gonzalez

1. Huntington Beach High School, Calif.
2. basketball
3. Oilers. The Chiefs traded their number 1, 3, 4 and 6 round picks for Houston's 1 and 4
4. seven, twice, both time against Jacksonville, on Nov. 9, 1997 and Sept. 13, 1998
5. 33
6. Walter White, who had 48 in 1977
7. 4
8. three, one for a touchdown

More Chiefs Trivia

Lamar Hunt

1. Geology
2. End
3. He traded quarterback Cotton Davidson to Oakland for their number one draft pick. The Texans used the pick to select Buck Buchanan.
4. 1972
5. The Chicago Bulls of the NBA and the Kansas City Wizards and Columbus Crew of Major League Soccer
6. Soccer and Tennis
7. Missouri and Texas

Hank Stram

1. Purdue
2. He was an assistant coach at the University of Miami, Purdue, SMU and Notre Dame.
3. 15 seasons
4. None
5. His game plan
6. Football and baseball
7. Five, in 1963 and 1974
8. Three, 1962 (Texans), 1966 and 1971
9. The New Orleans Saints
10. Broadcasting, doing TV and radio coverage of NFL games

Gunther Cunningham

1. Munich Germany
2. Allan Hancock College
3. Linebacker/Placekicker
4. Defensive line coach at Oregon
5. Four, Oregon, Arkansas, Stanford and Cal-Berkley
6. With the Hamilton Tiger-Cats of the CFL. He was the defensive line/linebackers coach
7. Three, the Colts, Chargers and Raiders
8. Twice, with the Raiders and Chiefs

Marty Schottenheimer

1. Pittsburgh
2. He was drafted by the Colts in the fourth round of the NFL draft and in the seventh round of the AFL draft by the Bills. He signed with the Bills.
3. Four: the Bills, Patriots, Steelers and Colts. He also played briefly with the Portland Storm in the WFL.
4. He worked in real estate.
5. The WFL's Portland Storm, linebackers coach
6. Giants, Lions and Browns
7. Eight games
8. Three times, 1985-1987
9. 1989
10. Three, 1993, 1995, 1997
11. 101
12. 145-85-1
13. 2-4
14. 3-7
15. 13, twice with the Chiefs, 1995 and 1997
16. Don Shula, Tom Landry, Chuck Noll and Bud Grant

The Playoffs

1. Oakland 2-1, Miami 0-3 and Buffalo 1-2
2. 8-11
3. Five
4. 14
5. Four – 1971, 1993, 1995, 1997
6. Three – 1962, 1966, 1969
7. No. They won the Super Bowl before the two leagues merged. They were AFL Champs and Super Bowl Champs in 1969.
8. John Alt, Tim Grunhard, Derrick Thomas and Dave Szott
9. Nick Lowery with 37 points in 8 games

10. Marcus Allen and Mike Garrett with three in six games
11. Barry Word, 130 vs. the Raiders on Dec. 28, 1991
12. Len Dawson with seven in eight games
13. 31, vs. Buffalo in the 1966 AFL Championship game
14. 41 to the Raiders on Dec. 22, 1968 in the Western Division playoff

1968 Divisional Playoff Game

1. KC and Oakland ended the season in a virtual tie
2. Five
3. Fred Biletnikoff, 7 receptions for 180 yards and 3 TDs
4. Jan Stenerud, 8-yard and 10-yard field goals
5. Four interceptions, all thrown by Dawson

1969 Divisional Playoff Game

1. The AFL adopted a one-year only playoff format for its last year of existence. The two division winners played the second place clubs from the other division in the first round. The two winners would then play for the AFL Championship.
2. 10-4
3. None
4. Four, three interceptions and one fumble
5. Marsalis had two, Thomas had one
6. Gloster Richardson on a 19-yard pass from Dawson in the fourth quarter
7. 23 yards in the second quarter, 25 in the third
8. Namath 14 of 40 for 164 yards, Dawson was 12-27 for 201 yards

1971 AFC Divisional Playoff Game

1. 82 minutes and 40 seconds
2. Both teams were 10-3-1
3. Podolak on a seven-yard pass from Dawson
4. Larry Csonka on a one-yard run
5. Three. From 29 yards, 31 yards and a 42 yarder was blocked
6. Miami had two, KC four
7. Wendell Hayes with 100 yards
8. Larry Csonka with 86 yards
9. Jim Otis on a one-yard run
10. 37 yards

1986 AFC Wild Card Playoff Game

1. While the Chiefs and Jets had the same record (10-6), the Jets won the tiebreaker for the home field.
2. Todd Blackledge, Bill Kenney was injured
3. The Chiefs' Jeff Smith, on a one-yard run
4. None
5. Albert Lewis recovered a blocked punt in the End Zone for the TD.

1990 AFC First Round Playoff Game

1. 12-4
2. Stephone Paige on 26-yard pass from DeBerg
3. Three
4. Mark Clayton on a 12-yard pass from Dan Marino
5. Okoye with 83 yards
6. 52 yards

1991 AFC First Round Playoff Game

1. The Chiefs were 10-6, the Raiders were 9-7
2. Todd Marinovich
3. Four
4. Fred Jones on a 11-yard pass from DeBerg
5. Three. He missed from 33 and 47 yards, and hit from 18.
6. Twice

1991 AFC Divisional Playoff Game

1. DeBerg and Vlasic
2. Three
3. Barry Word and Fred Jones
4. Denver. They won 10-7.

1992 AFC First Round Playoff Game

1. Yes, twice. 24-10 in San Diego and 16-14 in KC
2. San Diego with a record of 11-5
3. Marion Butts on a 53-yard run
4. Dave Krieg
5. Seven times for minus 43 yards

1993 AFC First Round Playoff Game

1. J. J. Birden on a 23-yard pass play

2. Allen with 67 yards
3. None
4. 46 seconds
5. Tim Barnett
6. 32 yards
7. Nine minutes and one second

1993 AFC Divisional Playoff Game
1. 30-0
2. Keith Cash on a seven-yard pass from Montana
3. Allen with 74 yards
4. Three
5. Nine
6. Allen on a 21-yard run

1994 AFC First Round Playoff Game
1. Houston, 31-9 and the Raiders, 19-9
2. 10-6
3. 17-17
4. Derrick Walker on one-yard pass from Montana
5. 64 yards
6. Two, an interception and a fumble

1995 AFC Divisional Playoff Game
1. San Diego
2. Jim Harbaugh
3. Lake Dawson
4. One, an interception by Mark Collins
5. Two, from 47 and 49 yards
6. 42 yards
7. Four, three interceptions and one fumble

1997 AFC Divisional Playoff Game
1. 12-4
2. They lost two fumbles.
3. Tony Gonzalez on a 12-yard pass from Grbac
4. 260 yards
5. Allen with 37 yards
6. 101 yards
7. Four times
8. Two minutes and 38 seconds

AFL & AFC Champ. Games

1962 AFL Championship Game
1. George Blanda
2. Dallas 17, Houston 0
3. Jack Spikes with 77 yards
4. Charley Tolar with 78 yards
5. 88 yards. He hit 9 out of 14 and had one TD pass.
6. 16 yards
7. Abner Haynes scored on a 28-yard pass from Dawson and a two-yard run.
8. 38
9. Five
10. Defensive end Bill Hull
11. 77 minutes and 54 seconds
12. 25 yards

1966 AFL Championship Game
1. War Memorial Stadium
2. Jack Kemp
3. Fred Arbanas on 29-yard pass from Dawson
4. Elbert Dubenion on a 69-yard pass play from Kemp
5. Otis Taylor on a 29-yard pass from Dawson
6. Johnny Robinson
7. KC 17, Buffalo 7
8. 253 yards and 2 touchdowns
9. Otis Taylor with 78 yards and a touchdown
10. Mike Garrett with 39 yards
11. Mike Garrett on runs of 1 and 18 yards
12. Seven, the Chiefs had four

1969 AFL Championship Game
1. 12-1-1
2. Charlie Smith on a three-yard run
3. Daryle Lamonica
4. Wendell hayes on a one-yard run
5. 129 yards. He was 7 out of 17
6. Wendell Hayes with 35 yards
7. Hewritt Dixon with 36 yards
8. KC 7, Oakland 7
9. Robert Holmes on a five-yard run
10. Three. George Blanda missed from 52, 39, 40 yards
11. Blanda
12. Four
13. 22 yards
14. Four times

1993 AFL Championship Game
1. Houston, 28-20
2. Buffalo's Thurman Thomas scored on a 12-yard run.
3. They were both from 31 yards.
4. 125 yards
5. Dave Krieg, 198 yards
6. Marcus Allen with 50 yards
7. Marcus Allen on a one-yard run

8. Three
9. Four
10. Keith Cash with six receptions for 87 yards

The Super Bowl

Super Bowl I

1. 63,036 (I'm going with this number because it's higher. Some record books have listed the attendance as 61,946.)
2. The Dallas Cowboys, 34-27
3. 12-2
4. The Mickey Mouse League
5. Jim Taylor
6. Curtis McClinton
7. Len Dawson with 24 yards
8. Taylor with 53
9. Green Bay's Max McGee on a 37-yard pass from Bart Starr
10. Curtis McClinton on a seven-yard pass from Dawson
11. GB 14, KC 10
12. Six, for 61 in losses
13. Buck Buchanan sacked Bart Starr
14. Three times for 22 yards in losses
15. Burford caught four passes for 67 yards
16. 17 yards on six attempts
17. Willie Mitchell
18. Max McGee, seven receptions for 138 yards and two touchdowns
19. Fred "The Hammer" Williamson
20. He was 16-27 for 211 yards.
21. Bart Starr

Super Bowl IV

1. The point spread was around 13, but as high as 17 or 18. They were generally considered to be a two-touchdown underdog.
2. 80,562
3. Cleveland, 27-7
4. 12-2
5. Joe Kapp
6. Mike Garrett with 39 yards
7. Bill Brown with 26 yards
8. Three times for a loss of 27 yards
9. Three times for 20 yards
10. Three, Lanier, Thomas and Robinson
11. 48, 32 and 25 yards
12. Mike Garrett
13. 65 Toss power trap
14. Otis Taylor, six catches for 81 yards
15. Henderson, seven receptions for 111 yards
16. Dave Osborne on a four-yard run in the third quarter
17. Taylor, on 46-yard pass play
18. KC 16, MIN 0
19. Gary Cuozzo
20. Four times
21. Len Dawson

Stadiums

Municipal Stadium

1. Nine
2. Muehlbach Stadium
3. Ruppert Stadium and Blues Stadium
4. The Kansas City Blues of the NFL in 1924, who became the Cowboys in 1925-26
5. Oct. 26, 1924. The Blues defeated the Rock Island Independents, 23-7.
6. Buffalo on Aug. 9, 1963 in an exhibition game
7. KC won, 17-13. 5,721 was the official attendance
8. 17,476 in 1923
9. 49,002
10. Buffalo, 22-9, on Dec. 19, 1971
11. 44-16-3 in regular season games

Arrowhead Stadium

1. Aug. 12, 1972. Pre-season Governor's Cup, Chiefs 24, Cardinals 14.
2. Three
3. Miami Dolphins receiver Marlin Briscoe on a 14-yard pass from Bob Griese on Sept. 17, 1972
4. Stenerud kicked a 40-yarder in the Miami game
5. Twice. 1995 and 1997
6. The Kansas City Wizards of Major League Soccer
7. 82,094 on Nov. 5, 1972 vs. Oakland
8. 1994
9. Two. Dec. 28, 1991, 10-6 vs. Oakland; Jan. 8, 1993, 27-24 vs. Pittsburgh

Other Stadiums

1. The Cotton Bowl
2. Abilene (1960), Midland (1961 and 1962) and Fort Worth (1961 and 1962). As the Chiefs, the team played in Fort Worth in 1964.
3. Veterans Field
4. Legion Field

5. Notre Dame

Uniforms

1. Red and white with gold trim
2. State of Texas with a star for Dallas
3. The helmet logo was changed.
4. 1960, all AFL teams wore their names on the back from the beginning of the league
5. White and gold trim was added to the sleeves on home jerseys, and red and gold trim on the away white jerseys.
6. 1968
7. AFL 10, a variation of the league's logo
8. 1988
9. They wore their white road socks at home.
10. It marked the 35th anniversary of the franchise.

Uniform Numbers

1. Numbers 16 and 28, worn by Len Dawson and Abner Haynes
2. Bill Maas. John Olenchalk and Marvin Terrell also wore number 63
3. Eight numbers—3, 16, 28, 33, 36, 63, 78, 86. Jan Stenerud, Len Dawson, Abner Haynes, Stone Johnson, Mack Lee Hill, Willie Lanier, Bobby Bell and Buck Buchanan
4. Three, Steve Bono, Wayne Clark, and Mark Vlasic
5. 3 and 16, both retired by the Chiefs
6. Cotton Davidson
7. Curtis McClinton
8. 18, Sean LaChapelle, Don Flynn and Elvis Grbac starting in 1999
9. 45
10. Mike Adamle, Bob Grupp, Durwood Pennington, Noland Smith, Matt Stevens
11. 83
12. 23

Quarterbacks

1. Cotton Davidson
2. Pete Beathard
3. Eddie Wilson
4. Bill Kenney and Todd Blackledge
5. Steve Bono
6. Len Dawson, 435 yards on Nov. 1, 1964 against Denver; Bill Kenney, 411 yards on Dec. 11, 1983 against San Diego
7. Steve DeBerg, 57.97%. Dawson is second at 57.22%.
8. Mike Livingston, 93 yards to Otis Taylor (last 14 yards were Robert Holmes, who received a lateral from Taylor) on Oct. 19, 1969
9. Joe Montana 55 (Oct.9, 1994 vs. San Diego) and Steve Bono 55 (Dec. 12, 1994 vs. Miami)
10. Three times. Don Merideth in 1960, Pete Beathard in 1964 and Todd Blackledge in 1983
11. Jacky Lee
12. Oct. 5, 1969 at Denver. KC won, 26-13.
13. SMU
14. Steve Fuller
15. Steve DeBerg-1991, Dave Krieg-1992 and Joe Montana-1993

Colleges

1. Otis Taylor and Jim Kearney, who are also cousins
2. Kansas
3. Mike Garrett and Marcus Allen
4. Pittsburgh
5. Ed went to Michigan State, Brad to USC.
6. Missouri
7. San Jose State
8. Northwestern
9. Grambling
10. Dino Hackett - Appalachian State
    Tim Grunhard – Notre Dame
    Frank Pitts – Southern (LA)
    Carlos Carson – LSU
    Neil Smith – Nebraska
    Pete Beathard – USC
    Barry Word – Virginia
    Jonathan Hayes – Iowa
    Nick Lowery – Dartmouth
    Gary Spani – Kansas State
    Bill Kenney – Northern Colorado
    Mike Bell – Colorado State
    Jerrel Wilson – Southern Mississippi
    Gary Barbaro – Nicholls State
    Emile Harry – Stanford

The Defense

1. 1968, 170 points
2. 1987, 388 points
3. 60, 1990
4. 37, 1968
5. -27, against Houston on Dec. 4, 1960
6. 330 by Pittsburgh on Nov. 7, 1976
7. -19, by the Chargers on Sept. 20, 1998
8. 499, by the Oilers on Dec. 16, 1990
9. Emmitt Thomas with 58
10. Derrick Thomas with 18

Running Backs

1. Christian Okoye with 4,897 yards
2. Curtis McClinton with 568 yards
3. Christian Okoye with 1,480 in 1989 and 1,031 in 1991, Joe Delaney with 1,121 in 1981, Mike Garrett with 1,087 in 1967, Tony Reed with 1,053 in 1978, Abner Haynes with 1,049 in 1962, and Barry Word with 1,015 in 1990.
4. Abner Haynes with 13 in 1962
5. Ted McKnight, against Seattle on Sept. 30, 1979.
6. Marcus Allen with 44
7. MacArthur Lane in 1976 with 66 receptions
8. Christian Okoye with eight in 1989
9. Twice, Abner Haynes in 1960 (875 yards) and Okoye in 1989 (1,480 yards)
10. Mike Garrett in 1967

Wide Receivers

1. Henry Marshall with 416
2. Carlos Carson with 80 in 1983
3. Otis Taylor with 57
4. Chris Burford with 12 in 1962
5. Frank Jackson caught four TDs against San Diego on Dec. 13, 1964.
6. Carlos Carson with 1,351 in 1983
7. Otis Taylor with 7,306 yards
8. Stephone Paige netted a then-NFL record 309 receiving yards against the Chargers on Dec. 22, 1985.
9. Carlos Carson, three times (1983-84, 1987), Otis Taylor – (1966 and 1971), Stephone Paige, 1990 and Andre Rison, 1997

Coaches

1. Paul Wiggin
2. Tom Bettis, seven games
3. Five, 1978-82
4. 31-42
5. Hank Stram, John Mackovic and Marty Schottenheimer
6. John Mackovic
7. Eight, including Gunther Cunningham
8. Two, Stram and Schottenheimer
9. nine

The Draft

1. Buck Buchanan and Ed Budde
2. Gale Sayers, who signed with the Bears
3. Otis Taylor-Prairie View, Frank Pitts-Southern, Gloster Richardson-Jackson State
4. Jim Marsalis, cornerback from Tennessee State
5. John Matusak
6. Paul Palmer-Temple
7. Willie Scott, TE from South Carolina
8. Bill Maas (NT – Pittsburgh) and John Alt (Tackle – Iowa)
9. Greg Hill
10. The seventh
11. Percy Snow in the first round and Tim Grunhard in the second

Kickers

1. Jack Spikes
2. Tommy Brooker
3. Mike Mercer from Buffalo
4. Cotton Davidson
5. Nick Lowery with 139 in 1990
6. 34 by Lowery in 1990
7. Jerrel Wilson with 46.1 yards per kick in 1965
8. Jerrel Wilson, with 43.6 yards per kick
9. Bob Grupp—74 yards against San Diego on Nov. 4, 1979
10. Five—Stenerud three times, Lowery four times. The most attempts in a game are seven by Stenerud on Dec. 19, 1971 against Buffalo
11. Bob Grupp with 11 against Baltimore on Sept. 2, 1979
12. Lewis Colbert with 99 in 1986
13. Jerrel Wilson with 1,014

What Position Did They Play?

1. Safety
2. Running back
3. Quarterback
4. Wide receiver
5. Tight end
6. Tackle
7. Linebacker
8. Defensive end
9. Safety
10. Guard
11. Defensive tackle
12. Fullback/Kicker
13. Wide receiver
14. Offensive tackle
15. Defensive back
16. Wide receiver
17. Wide receiver
18. Nose tackle
19. Running back
20. Defensive back

Nicknames

1. Fred Williamson
2. Sherrill Headrick
3. Mack Lee Hill
4. Cho Cho
5. Willie Lanier
6. Junious
7. Noland Smith
8. Barry Dean Hackett
9. Emil Joseph
10. Robert Holmes

Whether it's in the parking lot, tailgating (above, with Lamar Hunt), or in the stands (below), fans are always there to support their Chiefs.

Photo Credits

Alan Barzee - back cover, 23, 24 top, 26, 27 top, 56, 60 top, 62-65, 66 top, 68, 71 bottom, 72, 73, 74 bottom right, 75-77, 79, 80, 83, 90, 121, 129, 131, 134, 137, 154, 156, 189, 190, 192 bottom left, 204 top left and bottom left, 207 top left and top right

Courtesy of Tommy Brooker - 14, 32, 33, 171

Corbis Bettmann - 13, 18, 20, 40, 101, 177-181, 185

The Kansas City Star - 34, 36, 48, 82, 122, 186, 194

Courtesy of Kansas City Chiefs - 15, 16 top, 18 top, 29, 35, 44 bottom, 187 top

Kansas Collection, University of Kansas Libraries - 22, 25, 47, 51-52, 53 top, 54, 57, 59, 60 bottom, 61, 66 bottom, 97, 117, 118, 126, 133, 164, 165, 187 bottom, 195, 196, 198

St. Louis Mercantile Library - 102

Topeka-Capital Journal - front cover, 16 bottom, 21, 24 bottom, 27 bottom, 38, 39, 41, 42, 44 top, 45, 46, 53 bottom, 55, 70, 71 top, 74 top left, bottom left, top right, 78, 86, 93, 94, 98, 105, 106, 110, 113, 114, 125, 150, 162, 163, 166-169, 172, 173, 174, 182-184, 192 top left, top right, bottom right, 197, 199, 207 bottom, 209

Trancendental Graphics - 31, 153

About the Author

Mark Stallard is a free-lance writer who lives in Overland Park, Kansas, with his wife Merrie Jo. Mark has written for *The Wichita Eagle* and has had his work appear in several publications. He is a member of the Professional Football Researchers Association. *AFL to Arrowhead* is his second book.